A History of Moseley

by

Alison Fairn M.A

In loving memory of my parents

A. S. Fairn M.I.C.E., M.I. Struct. E.   **A. G. Fairn**
(1891 - 1972)   and   *(1895 - 1973)*

ACKNOWLEDGEMENTS

I would like to thank Mrs. G. M. Clarke, particularly for her help in transcribing the Moseley wills and inventories at Worcester County Record Office and at the Public Record Office, London, and for many discussions of the subject matter.

I am indebted also for information and assistance given by Mrs. M. Eccleston, Dr. N. Dyson, Dr. R. J. Hetherington, Miss B. Morris, J. W. Nunn, Lt. Col. J. C. Piggott, Miss J. M. Piggott, Mrs. E. N. P. Speed, Mr. R. Richardson, Mr. D. Swain, Mrs. A. Winstone, Mrs. D. J. Wright, Miss K. A. Wishart and also to Miss M. Henderson of Worcester County Record Office and the staff of the Local Studies Department of Birmingham Central Reference Library.

Alison Fairn

Together with a supplement covering the years 1970 - 2004, written by Moseley people and edited by John Williams

Published in 2004
by the 600 Celebrations Committee
St. Mary's Church, Moseley, Birmingham

This volume falls into two parts.

Part One (copyright Alison Fairn) contains a transcript of Alison
Fairn's original book, published in 1973.

On the inside front cover, there is a contents page for **Part Two** of the
book (copyright various authors as noted at the end of each article);
this consists of a series of articles describing various aspects of
Moseley life over the last 34 years.

All profits from sale of this book will go to the 600 Celebrations
Committee; the Committee wishes to extend their profound thanks to
all who have given their time to produce this book.

We also wish to acknowledge invaluable help with photographs from
James Hutchison, Roy Cockel, Fiona Ritchie and David Edgar

Designed and Printed by
The Art of Subtleties

Front Cover:
*Upper photograph taken in 1870, lower photograph taken in 2004 (by James
Hutchison)*

Back Cover:

Background picture - The Village Green taken in 1951

*Top - Photograph of Highbury Hall at the time when it was the home of Joseph
Chamberlain*

Centre - Moseley Dovecote, restored by the Moseley Society

*Bottom - Fred Lanchester, the first British car manufacturer, lived at 128 Oxford
Road,Moseley from 1923 until his death in 1946. The centenary of his first car was
celebrated in 1995; here are two 1921 40 HP Lanchester models, the one of the left a
Tourer, the other a Limousine, which were assembled for this memorable event.*

FOREWORD
to the 1973 Edition

Just three miles from the Centre of the second largest city in the country there stands, to the long established resident - "the Village"; to the newcomer - an "enigma".

To both it shows two faces; modern affluence and extreme poverty rest side by side, providing a testing ground of human relationships and understanding.

At the heart of the Village stands the village green, returfed yet shrinking each year, and overlooking the green, the Parish Church, described by one writer as "the Church on the hill which tells a city's history." Its tower is one of the oldest examples in the Midlands of brick faced with stone, and if those stones could talk they would tell a chequered tale of all that has gone on around it down through the centuries.

That we can now share in that tale is a privilege afforded us by Miss Alison Fairn, a local graduate history teacher and honorary Librarian of the Parish Church, who two years ago accepted my invitation to write a "History of Moseley". Modern Moseley is something of a writer's dream, but its history has been somewhat neglected, and Miss Fairn has needed to carry out a great deal of original research to present her narrative.

Miss Fairn has lived in Moseley for most of her life. Sometime a social worker, her writing shows an interest in people and their needs. She has deliberately used the "story form" as being the most effective way of presenting her subject. Her booklet is balanced, her style precise, yet easy to read.

She makes no attempt to analyse the second half of this century, but rather invites her readers to write their own last chapter on "the Victorian suburb that remains young at heart," perhaps because it is a unique mixture of life styles of generations and of colour; a "Village" which in more senses than one stands at the cross roads.

Lorys M. Davies
Vicar of Moseley.

November 1973.

A Preface to the new edition of 'A History of Moseley'

In the last paragraph of his foreword to the 1973 edition of this history, the Revd. Lorys Davies, then Vicar of Moseley, suggested that Alison Fairn had left the last chapter open, inviting her readers to make their own comments on the changing character of Moseley in the second half of the twentieth century.

More than thirty years have elapsed since that edition, giving time for considered reflection and analysis, and it seemed fitting to try and write that last chapter. It says something of the diversity and richness of Moseley life that the 'last chapter' became a much extended account, looking not only at the demographic changes, but also at the people of interest and significance who have lived in Moseley over these past fifty years, especially the 'Moseley scientists' who have merited a section of their own. The 'last chapter' also includes a section on the changing nature of leisure and the opportunities which Moseley offers.

At the heart of the 'village' is still the village green, adjacent to the shops and the public houses, close to a number of different bus routes facilitating transport, and still overlooked by the Parish Church of St Mary. In 1405 a papal mandate permitted the building of the original chapel of ease of St Mary, Moseley, and giving the people of the village their own place of worship instead of having to make the long and sometimes difficult journey on foot to Kings Norton church. In the year 2005 in which Birmingham diocese celebrates the centenary of its establishment, St Mary's celebrates the 600th anniversary of her foundation. The publication of this updated version of the 'History of Moseley' is one of the ways in which the church is commemorating her long involvement within the village of Moseley.

For many people, religion no longer plays a significant part in their everyday lives. Yet I believe that the churches and their resources of music, spirituality and community service still have much to offer to our increasingly secular society. At the same time we need to be willing to meet with those of other faiths and to build bridges of respect and understanding.

Moseley has been described as a 'melting pot', a place of diversity which reflects the diverse nature of the world in which we live. We can enjoy this rich diversity or retreat into our separate cliques and interest groups. The choice is ours; what that choice represents is of global significance.

Averyl Bradbrook
Vicar of Moseley

September 2004

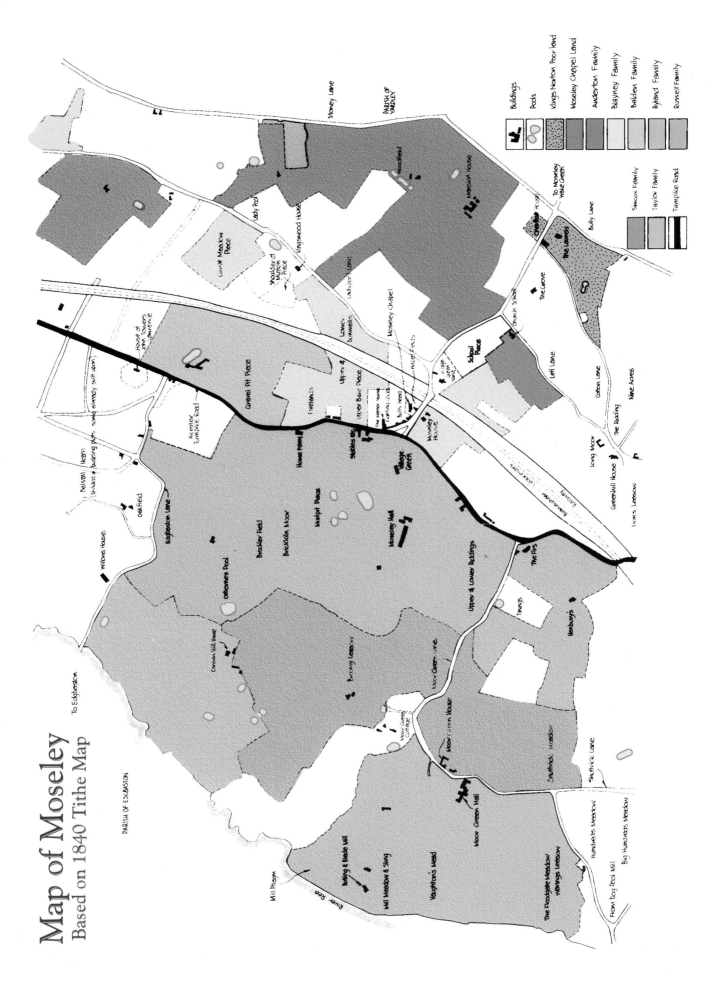

Map of Moseley
Based on 1840 Tithe Map

PARISH OF EDGBASTON

To Edgbaston

Legend:
- Buildings
- Pools
- Kings Norton Poor land
- Moseley Chapel land
- Anderton Family
- Blayney Family
- Belden Family
- Ryland Family
- Russell Family
- Smcox Family
- Taylor Family
- Turnpike Road

CHAPTER I.

THE FIRST INHABITANTS

M.W. ECCLESTON. 73.

Modern Moseley is a busy suburb of the vast City of Birmingham, a crowded area of Victorian and modern houses and shops clustered around roads noisy with heavy traffic. Its contemporary problems are those of an industrial urban area so most newcomers are amused when it is called "the Village" and few know that until this century it really was a village set attractively on a hill among woods and farms which the elderly still describe vividly. It has never been nationally well known but its history is a fascinating commentary on the lives of ordinary people affected by major events but steadily developing local resources and a satisfying community pattern.

Moseley cannot claim any definite link with the Romans, although there are suggestions that its clay may have been used in the Alcester kilns. It seems likely that Saxons were the first to realise the suitability of the dry bench of land for an agricultural settlement. According to the Ordnance Survey Map, the Alcester Road - Moor Green Lane junction is the highest point in modern Moseley at 524.4 feet above sea level. The soil is light and mostly well drained. There are deposits of gravel but also of clay. Plentiful supplies of water were available from springs and from the rivers Rea and Cole nearby. There were probably abundant trees for building purposes as the area lay on the edge of what was to be known as the Forest of Arden.

The Saxon hamlet was doubtless tiny but near the modern sites of St. Mary's Church and the Parade. The houses would have timber frames supporting wattle and daub walls and thatched roofs. Probably the common fields were small and the first settlers would have had little interest in the poor land of Balsall and Kings Heaths, to the North and South respectively, or the marshy Wake and Moor Greens to East and West.

On the Tithe Map of 1840 Hundreds Meadow and Big Hundreds Meadow are marked in the triangle now defined by Moor Green Lane, Dad's Lane and Shutlock Lane. This may have been the meeting place of a hundred Court which dealt with taxation, the maintenance of peace and the settlement of local pleas in the Saxon period.

The name Moseley is evidently Old English in origin. As the centre of settlement stands on high ground and the Domesday Book spelling was "Museleie", the first name was probably "mus(a)-leage", meaning "field-mice clearing". The old English word "moss" would suggest "bog clearing" as in the "Moseley" found in another part of Worcestershire, but the name "Moselege" in connection with our village first occurs in 1221, so this is an unlikely derivation.

The forefathers of the first inhabitants were Hwicce, who are believed to have been West Saxons who began to occupy South Worcestershire in the last two decades of the sixth century A.D. Bromsgrove was the mother settlement for our area and it seems likely that its inhabitants founded what we know as Kings Norton and that Moseley was colonised from the latter. In the Domesday Book William the Conqueror is described as holding "Bremesgrove ' in demesne with its eighteen berewicks, which included "Museleie" and "Nortune". The whole manor lay then in the Came Hundred, but by 1176 it was described in a Pipe Roll as being in the Hundred of Halfshire.

Although Nortune became a separate manor in the thirteenth century and was named Kings Norton in the fourteenth century, it descended with Bromsgrove until 1564 and remained royal until 1804 when John Taylor purchased it, and therefore Moseley, from the Crown. In the interim its resources were enjoyed by various noblemen, favoured by the contemporary monarch, until it was acquired by the powerful Mortimer family in the mid thirteenth century. The eighteenth century historian Nash believed that it reverted to the Crown again as the result of a marriage between Edward Mortimer, Earl of March, and Philippa, grand-daughter of Edward III and ancestress of Edward IV. Frequently the manor was held by queen consorts as in 1494 when Henry VII's queen Elizabeth gave land at Moseley on which a chapel might be built; in 1537 when Jane Seymour was named in a land case, and in 1629 when Henrietta Maria displeased local land holders by trying to enclose the waste.

Various local historians have believed that the Cistercians of Bordesley Abbey, near Redditch, founded a chantry chapel in Moseley, either in the area which was to become Chantry Road in the 1890's or as a forerunner of the parish church of St. Mary's. Certainly this religious community owned a grange in Kings Norton in the 13th century and in 1514 a Court case dealt with a dispute between the Abbot of Bordesley and the Prior of Worcester over payment of tithes thereon. The grange was listed among the Abbey's possessions at the Dissolution. Therefore at least there is proof of a connection with the area, but the records of Bordesley Abbey were lost and there is no evidence of a chapel building existing in Moseley before the sixteenth century, even in the sixteenth century historian Dugdale's "Monasticon".

Probably there was no chapel in the hamlet and its people were expected to attend Mass in the church at Kings Norton, which was dependent on Bromsgrove and in that parish until 1846, but which existed at least from the reign of Henry III, which ended in 1272. The journey via Moor Green Lane would often be unpleasant as the road was a mere track affected by the weather. There they may have seen the Bishop of Worcester as Moseley lay in that diocese until 1904.

The boundaries of Moseley seem vague to us until the parish of St. Mary's was created in the mid-nineteenth century. The hamlet developed in one of the original four tax yields of the Manor of Kings Norton. This Moseley Yield was rather irregular in shape. In modern terms its boundary line ran along Broad Lane, Kings Heath, to Yardley Wood Road, then northwards up Hollybank Road and Billesley Lane in the direction of Stoney Lane. It continued along that road to its junction with Highgate Road, then turned westwards by that and Belgrave Road to the bank of the River Rea. Its waters then bounded the Yield on the West. The settlement of Kings Heath eventually developed within this area also. The map was further complicated by the fact that what was known as "Moseley in Yardley" lay to the east of modern Billesley Lane, Belle Walk and Stoney Lane. This was in the parish of Yardley, in the County and diocese of Worcestershire, but presumably the inhabitants had social links with Moseley Village rather than more distant but more important Yardley.

CHAPTER II.

MOSELEY IN THE FIFTEENTH AND SIXTEENTH CENTURIES - PROSPERITY AND RELIGIOUS CHANGE

As the manor of Kings Norton was held by absentee royalty or great tenants-in-chief without local interests, there was plenty of scope for industrious yeomen to develop their resources and to achieve the status of gentry.

The Grevis or Greves were such a family who had become prosperous by the fifteenth Century. They probably had a large half-timbered farmhouse between modern Chantry and Salisbury roads which survived in part until 1842, according to the nineteenth Century antiquaries W. S. Brassington and Thomas Bickley. In 1468 one Thomas Grevis was of standing which enabled him to join the Guild of St. Anne at Knowle in Warwickshire. In 1520 another Thomas Grevis was elected Master of this society.

The Guild is interesting to us because so many Moseley people were members, although the guild hall and chapel were some 10 miles away. It was founded by Walter Cook, a canon of St. Paul's, London who died in 1423, for the mutual aid, benefit and protection of the members. They maintained a chapel where Mass might be said for the salvation of their own and their dead relations' souls. It was probably best supported between 1497 and 1506.

Several other Moseley families were named in the membership register:

John and Katherine Hawkis in 1492; John and Agnes Ayleston, Nicholas Bawnbroke and his wife, Richard and Elizabeth Bedill, Humphrey and Alice Rotton, Thomas and Joanna Welde and the priest William Bownell in 1495. In 1511 Moseley was represented by John and Elizabeth Bourne, Thomas and Alice Bissaker, Richard Webbe and Richard and Elizabeth Welld but in 1520 by Richard Rotton alone. If it is accepted that spelling of surnames varied according to choice until long after this period, the fortunes of some of these people's families may be followed in various legal documents discovered by W. B. Bickley. Nicholas Barnebroke was a witness in 1512 and possibly one of his family moved to Hinckley, Leicestershire, as in 1543 one John Barnebroke of Hinckley made grants of land in Moseley. In 1559 a Humfrey Barnebroke is mentioned. The Bedills' line is probably seen in the Richard Bydull who was a witness in 1446, the Roger Bedull granted land in 1491, the Richard Bedeill who rented Richard's Meadow in 1543 and in a yeoman and craftsmen who made wills between 1559 and 1639 which are still extant. Men named "William Hawkes" were witnesses in 1491, 1512 and 1589. Rottons are mentioned in 1512, when one Humphrey was a witness, and they frequently appear as wealthy yeomen. The farmer Ambrose Rotton who built Stratford Place outside the Manor in Camp Hill in 1601 was probably a relative of the Moseley Rottons, whose wills made between 1525 and 1632 indicate that they must have challenged the Grevis family's social position though described as yeomen.

Unfortunately there is little evidence to tell us how long or to what extent the Open Field System existed in the area or which families owned what farms, but there are references in various legal documents of the fifteenth and early sixteenth centuries to fields known as Cokrlytfyldis, Hemeryes, Lightmoor, Oldefeld, Richardsmedow, Shytterokk, Stockwell, Wardesmedow and Wyllyotts. Perhaps the second became the site of The Henburys, a large house opposite Valentine Road on the Alcester Road which was demolished in the late 19th century and Shytterokk may have been the modern Shutlock Lane. The other locations are lost or uncertain.

These families developed a prosperous community in the Moseley area in the late fifteenth, sixteenth and seventeenth centuries. Wills and inventories made by more than 50 individuals may be read in Worcester Record office and some Grevis wills in the Record office in London. On the death of anyone possessing even limited property his will and an inventory of his goods and chattels were sent to the consistory court of the diocese. If his estates and other possessions lay in more than one diocese the documents were sent to Canterbury. Technically all land in a manor belonged to its lord but customary procedure developed to facilitate transfer of any holding from a freeholder to his heir. According to an Elizabethan account of the customs of the Manors of Bromsgrove and Kings Norton a freeholder's death had to be reported by four other tenants at the first manorial Court held after it occurred. The deceased's heir then paid a heriot of 2/6, swore fealty to the lord of the manor and was admitted as the new tenant. Consequently land is rarely mentioned in Moseley wills. Probably many other such documents have been lost, so generalisations are dangerous. Yet as one touches the oddly assorted pieces of parchment and reads the cramped script many fascinating impressions are given of the testators' ways of life and even of individual characters.

The Richard Grevis whose will was made in December 1600 is described as a gentleman. Other sources indicate that in 1523 the head of the family had obtained a grant of arms described as "Argent on a fess azure, between three pellets, each charged with a lion's head erased of the field a griffon passant, between two escallop shells or. Crest a squirrell sejeant bendy sinister of four, argent and sable, holding between his paws an escallop shell or." His bequests make it evident that he held land not only in Moseley but also in Berkswell, Coventry and Sheldon and controlled "Borseley" (Bordesley) tithes and rectories and the parsonages and tithes of Sowe, Anstey and Shilton. A sister and a daughter had married men who lived at a considerable distance in contemporary terms: Richard Grene of "Wikene", Coventry, and Richard Parkes of Wednesbury. His standard of living is probably suggested by his bequest to his eldest son Richard of "my beste neste of gobletts duble guylte with the cover, and my best Salte double gylte, with the cover thereof, and my three cruses, with the footes, Stopper and cover thereof of double guilte, and my twelve sylver spoones of the Apostles and one little white sylver cope (cup)". He left £8 each to his daughters Isabel King and Dorothy Parkes, £100 among other bequests to his son Thomas, 40/-to his servant John Howle and 6/8 each to all other servants. The poor of Kings Norton were to receive 30/- and those of Moseley twelve pence for each poor household. Twenty marks were to be distributed at his burial.

An interesting glimpse of family problems is given by the clauses which bequeath property in Berkswell to Thomas "without interference from Anne his wife" and make the same lady a residuary legatee and executrix" if she leaves Thomas in peace"!

Unfortunately the inventory which must have been made of Richard Grevis' goods has not survived but that of another local gentleman did. Thomas Greene of Moseley died in 1589 and we can learn much about him from the vivid details. His goods were worth about £228 altogether. In his house were a hall, parlour, inner parlour, buttery and inner buttery. There were chambers over the buttery, the inner parlour and the hall and a chamber beneath the hall. He had also a kitchen and outhouses. The glass in the windows was valued at 26/8d. The usual furnishings of a comfortable Elizabethan home are listed in profusion with the carpets, curtains, painted cloths and specialised vessels etc. which might be expected of his status. He even had forks, a luxury in the sixteenth century. His treasures included a silver salt without a cover, two of gilt with covers, gilt goblets and cups. The clothes included in the inventory were two gowns, a jacket, four coats, four doublets, hats, caps, etc. but one suspects that his servant may have helped himself beforehand. Evidently Thomas Greene used his land for mixed farming. He grew rye, barley and oats and kept cattle, horses and oxen. Members of his household spun thread and wove cloth, made butter, cheese and beer, and ground grain. All the necessary equipment is listed. Unfortunately there is no evidence of where he lived or of his relatives and heirs as his will has been lost.

He was probably related at least distantly to John Greene, the tanner who died in 1586 and left chattels worth £128.13. 10, a considerable sum. Certainly a Thomas Greene was one of the overseers of the will. As the leaders of the community seem to have risen from the ranks of yeomen, such relationship must have been common and may have contributed to community unity. John's clothes were worth 26/- and he left his best coat to his brother. His house consisted of hall, three chambers, kitchen and outhouses. In his inventory, as in all the others, much stress was laid on the three types of sheet: flaxen, hempen and noggon. He had one painted cloth and six cushions but three silver spoons were probably his most valued possessions. As was usual for an Elizabethan tanner he also farmed as 5 oxen, many kyne, 4 horses, 5 swine, sheep and poultry are listed. He left 3/4d to Moseley Chapel and 12 pence to each of the 12 poorest householders in the village, as well as his clothes.

George Watson was a bladesmith who died in 1552 and whose goods were worth £58.1 1.0. His premises included a mill in which were found "greate stones" worth £3.10.0., which were probably grind stones driven by the mill wheel. In his parlour hung a sword and dagger worth 3/4d. and in the storehouse were moulds, bellows, iron, steel and coal. Perhaps the mill was on the site by the Rea where similar buildings stood until Holder's Mill was demolished in 1957. Watson or his family kept seven cattle, grew corn and rye, and made cheese.

Other craftsmen were the smith John Watton, Richard Bydle the weaver and Richard Byddle the wheeler, whose wills were proved in 1552, 1559 and 1585. Their homes held eight, six and four looms respectively and they were all involved in mixed farming. Watton evidently treasured his bellows as one pair was given to his elder son and the other to his younger. The weaver was concerned about his furred gown and the wheeler allocated his timber and tools carefully. Their chattels were worth £21.18.5., £10.12.4., and £16 respectively.

The Richard Rotton who died in 1588 was a yeoman who seems to have been poor, though presumably related to the very prosperous local Rotton family, as he left chattels worth only £15.2.3. His house included hall and parlour, three chambers and a kitchen, buttery, smithy and outhouses but he had only four cattle. His clothes were worth 16/- and his treasure was four silver spoons. Perhaps he was the grandson of yeoman John Rotton whose will was proved in 1575 and who bequeathed single spoons to each of his five children and to two others. At least John also remembered Moseley Chapel, unlike Watton and the Byddles.

Moseley was still part of the Manor of Kings Norton and subject to its institutions. Since mediaeval times the larger area had been controlled by a bailiff, constable and reeve elected by the tenants at the Court Leets held annually on the Thursday in Whit week. Each of the 5 elds or yields, of which Moseley was one, would have its own ale taster and a third borough or constable, whose task of conserving the peace was symbolised by the staff fixed outside his door.

Yet Moseley must have developed a sense of its own identity early as in February 1405 Pope Innocent VII sent a mandate to the Bishop of Worcester to licence a chapel of Saint Mary, Moseley, for Mass and other divine offices. This was the result of a petition claiming that Kings Norton Church was so distant that for old men, pregnant women and other weak persons access was impossible, especially when there were floods. Presumably a small chapel was erected in Moseley soon afterwards but no remains of it are visible today. It may have been a simple half-timbered building. In 1494-5 Henry VII's queen Elizabeth of York, in her capacity of lord of the Manor of Kings Norton, made a formal grant of certain waste lands as a site for a chapel but the clergy of Kings Norton continued to care for the inhabitants, who were to remain in that parish until 1853. Moseley baptisms and burials were registered at Saint Nicholas Church until 1758 and marriages until 1853. Services of marriage and burial and the actual committals took place in the mother church and churchyard until the late eighteenth century.

In 1446 John Shyngler was described as Chaplain of Moseley when he witnessed a document and Dominus William Bownell of the Guild of St. Anne in 1495 was obviously one of his successors. He must have been much concerned with the erection of St. Mary's Tower.

The early seventeenth century writer Thomas Habington stated in his "Survey of Worcestershire" that the steeple of Moseley was "begun to be buylded" in 1513 and dedicated to Our Lady by John Wednesbury, Prior of Worcester" at the instant labor of John Middelmore of Haselwell, Sir William Bownell, Chaplayne to Our Lady at Moseley, Humfrey Rotton, Thomas Greene and William Hawkes". According to the Prattinton MS. written in Henry VIII's reign, the necessary stone was brought in 48 loads from the walls of the ruined Parsonage of Bromsgrove. In 1523 Alice Middlemore left instructions in her will for her son to give a suitable sum for the repair of the chapel and steeple of Moseley. On the wall at the West-End of the church, above the arch which opens into the Tower, there may be seen the marks of the roofs of the churches built in 1514, 1780 and 1824. The first indicates that it belonged to a small, low building but it must have been a great source of pride to the villagers.

In 1548 the hamlet was affected by events of national importance. The young Protestant Edward VI appointed commissioners to survey chantries and free chapels and these men visited Kings Norton, if not Moseley itself. Their report read "That the said paryshe is II myles brode every waye & fortie myles compass and that many of the same parishe do dwell foure myles from the parishe church and therefore is one Chappell buylde by the Paryshoners there at a village called Moseley where that Sir Lawrence Blackeway doth mynster sacraments and other necessarye usages in ye said chapel to dyvers the inhabitants of the said parishe, dwelling near to the said Chappell, which is two myles dystante from the said parishe Churche". Lawrence Blackeway was described as "of the age of 30 and syx yeres, learnyd & of honest convasacon". The title "sir" suggests that he was not a graduate.

Edward VI eventually granted adequate resources for the maintenance of the clergy and altars in Kings Norton and Moseley to a group of trustees. According to a list made in 1729 of benefactions to Moseley Chapel he also granted 14 nobles p.a. from the audit money paid in Worcester on the Monday after Michaelmas.

In 1552 an inventory of church furniture was made on the same king's orders. Evidently John Butler was then the curate in charge of Moseley Chapel and had the use there of one silver chalice and paten, one pair of old white camelot vestments, two altar cloths and two towels, two small brass candlesticks and three bells. It was noted that the sanctus bell had been sold. It was not required in Protestant services.

In 1553 Edward was succeeded by his devout Roman Catholic sister Mary. Fortunately for Moseley her servants also found "the Chapel of Our Lady necessary to continue," so she and her husband, Philip II of Spain granted a new charter in 1558 to ensure the continued existence of the chapel with the provision that Lawrence Blackeway should continue in the place of minister there and that he should have £4.13.0. as yearly salary. It would seem that receipt was irregular as it was necessary to petition the Barons of the Exchequer to order the payment of arrears.

There is little evidence to indicate the reaction of Moseley's inhabitants to the Reformation. Probably their real loyalty was to their chapel and usually to the curate serving it whatever the form of service and its doctrinal basis. Busy with the practical problems of daily life, they may not have been fully aware of the changes in their own practice and belief. Late in Henry VIII's reign yeoman John More bequeathed his soul "unto Almighty God to be with our Lady Seynt Mary and all the blessed company of heaven". and Richard Webb's will referred to "our blessyd Lady Seynt Mary". In 1546 Agnes Webb left the residue of her estate to her son-in-law "to dispose of as he thinks fit for the welthe of my soull". Yet John More in the tenth year of Elizabeth's reign merely referred to the maintenance of "God's servys in Moseley" for which he left 3/~ and the extreme Protestant element was to be particularly Strong in the area by the 1620's.

Bequests for the maintenance of the chapel were frequently made. In 1558 Humphrey More, yeoman, left 6/8d. In 1562 Richard Welde left 16d and in 1586 John Greene, tanner, left 3/4d. Knowle and Moseley landowner Humphrey Greswolde's bequest in 1570 was of ten shillings and Thomas Greene allocated the same sum in 1589. Richard Grevis left a further ten shillings in 1600 specifically for repairs to the building. In his will he left another ten shillings. As he also subscribed £25 to the Armada Defence Fund in 1588 he was presumably a loyal subject of Protestant Elizabeth 1, and the local community probably followed his lead.

CHAPTER III.

MOSELEY IN THE SEVENTEENTH CENTURY - PARLIAMENT AND PRESBYTERIANISM.

The first great house to be built on the site of modern Moseley Hall was probably planned by the Richard Grevis who inherited in 1601. He was the most successful of the family and evidently found favour with James I or Charles I as his will of June 1632 refers to his "free warraunte" of Yardley, Worcestershire, and Solihull, Warwickshire, "lately graunted to me and my heires by the King's Majesty". He also held land in Bicknell, Layndon, Castle Bromwich, Little Bromwich, "Borseley and Sutton Colfel I", Lee in Yard ley and Sheldon. He was knighted in 1604, High Sheriff of Worcestershire in 1616 and a magistrate who doubtless virtually ruled Moseley.

The Records of Worcester Quarter Sessions between 1607 and 1631 list the many and varied cases which he considered. For instance in 1607 Sir Richard bound over John Carelesse, Bromsgrove shoemaker, on his own recognizance and those of 2 others that he would appear "to answer for getting Grace Cottrell of Moseley with child". In 1619 it was the turn of Thomas Hunt of Kings Norton who was accused of selling ale without a licence and allowing unlawful games on the Sabbath. In the same year he bound over Edward Brecknall of Birmingham to keep the peace against Edward Broom of Moseley. Although Sir Richard's surname was spelt in the Session halls as "Greves", "Grevys" and "Greaves" his own signature was "Greves".

Sir Richard left 40/- to the 40 poorest householders in Moseley, the same amount as he left to his daughter Merrall for a mourning ring. Unfortunately the inventory of his household goods has not survived.

It may be significant that he left no money to Moseley Chapel. The Reverend Thomas Hall of Kings Norton referred to him in 1651 as "a valiant and religious man" who sheltered nonconformist ministers.

The Arms of Grevis of Moseley granted 1523

After his death a magnificent tomb was erected in St. Nicholas' Church Kings Norton, where it still stands. He is represented wearing armour, lying beside the effigy of his wife, Anne Leighton of Wattlesborough, Salop. Figures of their four sons and four daughters kneel either side of the laudatory inscription on the wall above. Above these are carved the Grevis arms impaled with those of Leighton, which are described as "Quarterly, per fesse indented or and gules". Their crest is "a wyvern wings expanded sable".

The epitaph is most impressive:

"Whom neither bribes nor servile feares have' swaide
From vertu's centur, in this urne is laid.
The aire was iustice that his bodie breathd
And peace his being till his soule had leaved
Being iust in peace, he spent his time, his paines
And therefore Iusdy now in peace he reignes.
His hart was fixed on heaven and he stood
Not for his owne but for his country's good.
His mind was nobly ballant, not to sell
His smile for wealth yet used his tallant well.
Wherefore his name hath broke detraction's fetters
And well abides the touch in golden letters."

It must have been difficult to succeed such a father as Sir Richard but his second son and heir Thomas was the Grevis who showed courage by refusing knighthood for a fee at the coronation of Charles I, for

Tomb of Sir Richard Grevis (died 1632) in St. Nicolas Church Kings Norton

which audacity he was fined £10 in 1632. In 1638 he opposed Queen Henrietta Maria in her role as Lord of the Manor of Kings Norton. She had sent Sir Thomas Hatton and others to "improve, sever and set out such part of the said waste grounds as they think fit and share the rent among the copyholders and other tenants and to ditch and empail the residue so that her Majesty might dispose thereof." It was eventually agreed by local landholders that the Queen should have a third of the land to be enclosed while the rest should be divided among the tenants, but in 1638 "Thomas Greves" joined other prominent local men such as John Middlemore and Richard Rotton in plotting "to deprive her Majesty of profit" and "advance their own without just or lawful title" by destroying the banks etc. which she had caused to be erected, claiming that use of the former waste lands appertained to their freehold and copyhold. In 1641 they were ordered to appear in the Court of Her Majesty's Revenue at Westminster, but subsequent events are obscure. In 1643 Parliament seized all royal estates, including the Queen's, as the Civil War had begun.

In 1639, as Sheriff of Worcestershire, Thomas Grevis was warned by the Privy Council to bring in the County's Ship Money. He probably considered the imposition illegal as this tax was supposed to be levied only on coastal towns and that in time of war or danger from the sea.

Mr. F. A. Bates, who compiled "Graves' memoirs of the Civil War" from seventeenth century sources, could not find much definite evidence of Thomas' further career. He must have been in financial difficulties as he borrowed money from John Whateley of Kings Norton, who forgave him a debt of over £300 in his will of 1638-39, and from his relative Sarah Greaves of Guildford, who died in 1640. He presumably supported Parliament when the First Civil War began in 1642 as his name appears on lists of those appointed by Parliament to collect money in 1643 and 1647. The last mention of his name in this connection was in 1648, so he may have been obliged to flee from England as his brother had displeased Oliver Cromwell. This would explain why the same brother, Colonel Richard Grevis or Graves, was in charge at Moseley Hall between 1652 and 1671.

This soldier was Sir Richard Grevis' fourth son, but spelt the surname "Graves". His career is well documented and fascinating. Presumably he grew up sharing the Presbyterian outlook of his father and he must have been influenced by his brother's opposition to Queen Henrietta Maria. He may have joined Lord Willoughby of Parham in 1642 to fight successfully against Prince Rupert near Birmingham. When the Prince returned there in March 1643 Graves was in command of defensive earthworks, from which he was soon forced to withdraw, but he and his men then charged from the Lichfield end of the town so effectively that the Earl of Denbigh was mortally wounded and the Royalist force withdrew from Birmingham. His obvious military ability made him well known and he was called to raise the Lord General's Own Regiment of Horse in 1644. Colonel Graves was loyal to Parliament and so eventually found himself in charge of Charles I at Holmby House, Northamptonshire, in 1647. Parliament was then anxious to disband the New Model Army, whose leaders were trying to seize power, and so Graves planned to escort the King to a place under Parliament's control. Oliver Cromwell foiled this move by sending Cornet Joyce to capture the royal prisoner, whose Moseley sympathiser eventually escaped to Holland in 1648 to join a group of exiled Presbyterians at Breda.

According to Mr. Bates, Colonel Graves there became a Groom of the Bedchamberto Charles II and accompanied him to Scotland to negotiate with the Scots Covenanters and the Kirk Party. Consequently he was involved in the fateful Battle of Worcester on September 3rd, 1651, and was captured by the Roundheads and sent to the Tower of London to await trial. A contemporary broadsheet bears a portrait of him which shows that he was dark haired and wore a moustache.

Fortunately, in 1652 he was allowed bail on condition that he stayed within five miles of his mother's Worcestershire home, presumably Moseley Hall. There he lived to become a magistrate in 1656. Presumably he was prosperous as the will of his wife Anne Henshaw lists three watches and a "torter shell cabinett with a black ebony frame" among other valuables. Their son Richard succeeded to the estate in 1681.

The Rottons were still flourishing. Yeoman John who died in 1620 left chattels worth £416.13.4. His house sounds spacious with its hall, parlour, six chambers and a special chamber for the storage of cheese. His clothes were worth £5. Like an Elizabethan gentleman he owned carpets and among his furniture are listed a desk and books worth 35/-. He had thirteen silver spoons, a silver and a gilt cup, a gilt salt, "a muskett and a birding piece". He used coal and grew wheat.

The Rachel Rotton who died in 1629 was probably his widow. Her rather overbearing personality makes an unpleasant impression three and a half centuries later. She was very conscious of her wealth, for as well as the Moseley chattels she owned houses in Wolverhampton which were to be enjoyed by each of her four daughters in turn for two years "making no manner of waste" and she made marriages approved by the executors a condition of her daughters' inheritance. Her goods were worth £198.5.5. including clothes at £5. She owned books valued at 40/- and a desk, possibly the one mentioned in John Rotton's inventory, and 10 silver spoons. She left a gold angel to each mother-in-law, Alice Rydley and Anne Rotton, a gilt cup to Sarah Willmott and 12 pence to each godchild. The poor of Kings Norton received 40/- and so did the poor of Wolverhampton. She left 5/- to each servant. A puritan or presbyterian outlook may be indicated by the fact that she gave nothing to Moseley Chapel but 10/- to the preacher who officiated at her funeral.

Her mother-in-law Anne, who made a will in 1628 but died in 1632, makes a much more attractive impression so one wonders how she fared at Rachel's hands and presumably in Rachel's house. Her chattels were worth £245.6.2. so perhaps Rachel was careful not to offend her. Her clothes were valued at £7. She left the furnishings of one bedchamber and many treasures, which had obviously been lent to friends and relatives to whom they were now bequeathed. She left silver salts to her son Richard, her cousin Joseph Smallbroke and to Walter Marston, green rugs to Sara Smallbroke, Alice Marston and Dorothy Rotton, linen to granchildren. Various female relatives received money to buy mourning clothes and there were many bequests of 5/-to each of Rachel's servants and 2/- to each of those of her other children, which suggests that she travelled around the family's houses. She allocated 20/- to the Birmingham poor, to be distributed by the Smallbrokes, and a silver penny to every poor person who might attend her funeral in Kings Norton. She left 10/- to the minister who was preaching and living in Moseley at her death.

The seventeenth century Byddles were represented by three wills of yeoman John, proved in 1607, weaver Humphrey, proved in 1611 and yeoman Roger, proved in 1639. The first left goods worth £90.5.6., including 40/- worth of clothes and 24 pieces of pewter, and the last left two grandsons £10 each and 12 pence a year to ten of Moseley's poorest inhabitants. Unfortunately his inventory is lost. Humphrey the weaver lett £1 3.0.9, his two looms to his sons, a brass pot to one of them and pans to his two daughters.

Other interesting wills are the very precise one of spinster Alice Forrest who left £26.1 3.4. to relatives in 1607, and that of the clergyman John Lyndon who died in 1618. He had very little furniture but his books were worth 30/-and he had three silver spoons.

Elizabeth Greaves, presumably the daughter of Thomas who inherited in 1632, left twenty pounds to be used for the poor of Moseley. She entrusted this task to her "loving friend" Master Fincher, the minister, and left mourning rings worth 20/- each to him and to the Reverend Thomas Hall. She died in 1654.

The last will of lively detail was that of John Moore, the whitesmith who died in 1686. Moores had lived in Moseley at least since the 1540's but most were probably yeomen. John seems to have been a bachelor or widower who left little furniture, only pewter utensils and goods worth £1 7.19.2. but he had a Bible and some other books, lands by the Rea and a blade mill. Perhaps he was a descendant of George Watson. This local industry must have been well sited.

It is not possible to judge how many of Moseley's inhabitants were of the same political opinions as the Grevis family, but there does appear to have been a noticeably nonconformist group in the village who probably sympathised with Parliament. It is noticeable that in 1628 and 1629 respectively Ann and Rachel Rotton had made wills bequeathing 10/- to whoever was the preacher in Moseley at the time of her decease rather than mentioning the chapel. The Reverend Thomas Hall of Kings Norton in a 1651 address to his parishioners referred to their enjoyment "in one part of the parish for almost fifty years together" of the services of" a succession of very eminent and able divines, conformable nonconformists, conformable to the canon of scripture though not to the Bishop's canons" and it is clear that he meant Moseley as he continued: "Where the Lord raised up that valiant and religious knight Sir Richard Grevis, who by his wisdom and courage sheltered these reverend ministers from these episcopal storms which otherwise had fallen upon them." One local historian lists eighteen men who would fit Hall's description besides himself, and who were chaplains at Moseley Hall so probably lived in and influenced the village.

Colonel Graves is believed to have invited Samuel Shaw to become minister of Moseley in 1657. He was a Presbyterian ordained at Wirksworth whom Hall described as having "so much excellence in a little body". In that year the Council of State approved a stipend of £25.6.8. for the minister of Moseley. By 1660 Joseph Cooper had taken Shaw's place. He must have been greatly appreciated because his income was the considerable sum of £50 p.a. thanks to parishioners' generosity. According to Edmund Calamy, the author in 1702 of "A particular account of the Ministers . . . who were silenced and ejected by the Act of Uniformity . . . " Cooper was a scholar of Latin, Greek and Hebrew and one who "hath often charmed a rude meeting into civil order and composed lewd persons into a proper decorum". Yet on a Sunday in 1662 he was evicted by a troop of horse from the very pulpit for refusing to accept the Book of Common Prayer and the Act of Uniformity. He went to live in Kings Norton and was there until 1672 at least.

A diocesan Census of 1676 credited Kings Norton with 1,058 Conformists, 19 Papists and only 5 Nonconformists. The few church-wardens' presentments which are available in Worcester Record Office inform us that though in 1684 there were no "schismatical meetings" in the parish "that wee doo know of" yet in October 1690 it was reported that there was a regular and orderly congregation at the parish church of St. Nicholas which would have been larger "if a course was taken to reform the abuse of Moseley Chapell, which is usually supplied every Sunday by one or other Nonconformist who have now formed themselves into a Club to take their turns there, the more effectually to decoy the people from their parish church". In June 1693 the churchwardens reported that "our chapell of Moseley is still intruded into by preachers refusing conformity to the Church of England as established by law, and that they prevent the licensed curate from performing his duty there to our general trouble and discouragement". In 1696 there was a further reference to "the abuse of the Chappel of Moseley where Nonconformists usually thrust in and preach", but at last in 1699 the minister of Kings Norton was described as preaching once a month "in Moseley Chapple ... where the Congregation behave themselves as orderly as in our Parish Church". If only the actual incidents had been recorded in what was probably dramatic detail.

These records also indicate that some families were Roman Catholics. No addresses were given but the name Anderton later became well known in Moseley. Quakers included Richard Niblett and John Bissel.

Conforming Curates in official charge of St. Mary's Chapel in the late seventeenth Century were John Burney B.A., (1680-84) William Woolaston M.A. (1684-86) and John Jones B.A. (1686-1701). The second of these was Second Master at King Edward VI's School, Birmingham, but he inherited "an ample estate" and settled in London to write. There is a copy of his "The Religion of Nature Delineated" on view in St. Mary's. Ten thousand copies of this work were sold.

During the seventeenth century two of three bells listed in the inventory of 1552 must have been recast. These were given to St. Anne's Church, Moseley, in 1875. The treble was inscribed "God Save the King, 1638"; the second with "Jesus bee our God Speed, 1650" and with a bell between the letters "IM", which probably stood for the bell founder John Martin of Worcester.

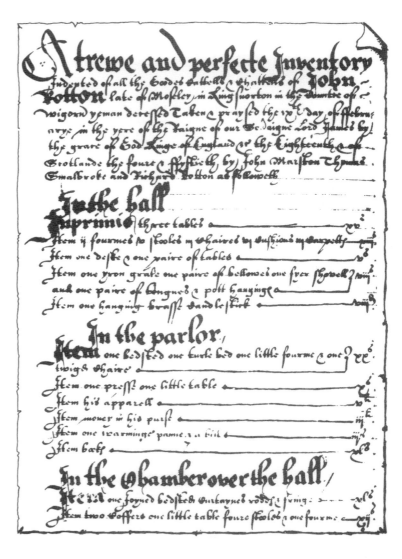

CHAPTER IV.

MOSELEY IN THE EIGHTEENTH CENTURY - ELEGANT EXPANSION

By the beginning of the eighteenth century Moseley was developing rapidly. The most prominent buildings must have been the church and the Grevis house but there were evidently several handsome half-timbered buildings in which families such as the Rottons had lived. In 1908 W. J. Spurrier listed farms of this type and period such as Swanshurst (1662), Fleetwood's off Anderton Park Road and Moorcroft. He also mentioned the introduction of brick in the construction of the Bull's Head Inn and adjoining cottages, other cottages in Cotton Lane, Billesley Lane and Lett Lane (later School Road) farmhouses in the areas of School Road, Springfield Road, Stoney Lane and Moor Green Road and large houses such as The Woodlands and Hayfields, which give their names to modern roads. Charlton Lodge at the corner of Cotton Lane, Wake Green House between St. Agnes Road and Billesley Lane, The Laurels and The Grove between Lett and Billesley Lanes the Manor House to the North of the modern King Edward's Road, and Moor Green House. Most of the farm land was enclosed in fields as only a little waste remained common until the Enclosure Act of 1772 and the area must have presented the pleasantly cultivated appearance of mixed farming. Field names of 1706 included Brierley Hill or the Gosty, Evenson Hill, Nether and Further Ashfields and Coxes Close.

At some time in the seventeenth Century rolling mills were established at Moor Green. The Jonathan Moore who died there in 1685 was a bladesmith. Doubtless there was a smithy in the village where farm implements and horseshoes were produced and repaired. There was also the site at Sarehole, which had been in use as a commill since the Middle Ages, but was leased by Matthew Boulton from 1756 to 1761 for rolling sheet metal. His successor Richard Eaves erected a new building where he ground cutlery and edge tools. Moseley people would also know the windmill on Wake Green which David Cox painted late in the century.

The roads connecting Moseley with Birmingham and Kings Norton would still be rough tracks so the community would be largely self-sufficient.

The Grevis family was in decline. The first record of financial problems since those of Thomas was made in 1688 and these were probably never completely solved. In that year yet another Richard died willing the sale of various land holdings and timber in Moseley to pay his debts.

Probably financial anxiety led to family strife. In 1727 Colonel Richard's third son, Benjamin Grevis, made a will in which he first piously committed his soul to God and then continued- "I give and bequeath unto my dear and loving wife Elizabeth Grevis all such part of the furniture of what kind soever the same, now standing ...in a certain chamber in Moseley Hall aforesaid commonly called the Nursery, and as was hers before her inter-marriage with me, and I also give and bequeath unto my said dear and loving wife the sum of twenty pounds". Revenge seems obvious but perhaps Elizabeth was no angel herself, as in 1743 she was involved in a legal dispute when trying to prevent payment of the beneficiaries of her son by a previous marriage. She thought that she had won and ordered the bells of Moseley to be rung but judgement was given against her next day.

Benjamin evidently had a poor opinion of his son Richard too. By the 1727 will he left him only the proverbial shilling and made Richard's sister Jane sole executrix. When her father died in 1729 she formally renounced this obligation in favour of her brother, possibly unwisely. In 1733 he was obliged to mortgage the Red Lyon Inn, of unknown site, and plots of land in Moseley to one Mary Worcester. Further properties which may have belonged to the Grevis family for centuries were offered for sale in the 1750's.

Richard's obituary in 1759 described him as "a gentleman of polite understanding, humane and courteous Deportment, who adorned private life with every amiable Virtue and cultivated a calm, universal benevolence for all Mankind", but one suspects that he was either naive or dominated by his wife Ann because his will provided first for her and then for his second son Charles, while the heir Henshaw was the residuary legatee. Unfortunately the residue was minimal so in 1761 the Moseley estates of the Grevis family were offered for sale. The Hall was evidently occupied by two families at the time. The sale also included Hill Farm, the Silver Rolling Mill, More's Green Farm, the Swan Inn let to John Strettill and land "above the Chapel."

The next record of Henshaw Grevis was made in 1786 when he must have been in sadly reduced circumstances, living in a back house in Edgbaston St., Birmingham and working as a gravel pit carter. He was summoned to

Birmingham Court of Requests for failing to pay a debt of 17/-. One of the magistrates, who remembered seeing him as a gaily dressed youth riding to hounds across Moseley Park, gave him the job of distributing "Aris' Gazette" in Leicestershire and he was thus employed until his death in 1788. He was buried as a pauper in Kings Norton church-yard as his children had died before him. His younger brother Charles had climbed as he fell because a successful military career, started in the Marquis of Lothian's Dragoons, led to marriage with an heiress. There are probably collateral descendants of the Grevis family in the Midlands to this day but their long connection with Moseley and Moseley Hall was at an end.

The estate was bought for £9,000 by John Taylor of Bordesley Park. He was a button maker with a factory in Union Street, Birmingham, who had made a fortune of £200,000. According to the contemporary historian and bookseller William Hutton, Taylor "possessed the singular power of perceiving things as they really were" and to him were owed "the gilt buttons, the japanned and gilt snuff boxes with the numerous race of enamels." He knew Matthew Boulton and his amazing circle of pioneer Midlands industrialists though himself born in London. He probably bought the Moseley estate as an investment as he never lived there and let the property to members of his family or friends.

His son John was a banker with interests in Birmingham and London. He became a magistrate and Deputy Lieutenant of Worcestershire. Although the Grevis Moseley Hall still stood, he built a brick and stone mansion at a cost of £6,000 after inheriting Moseley Park in 1775. The style was simple: a three storeyed building linked by low wings to outhouses at either side.

In the last quarter of the eighteenth century other Birmingham businessmen bought property in Moseley. Of course it was conveniently near the industrial town where their factories and workshops lay and it was a pretty, healthy place. The old road to Birmingham would have been a disadvantage. As late as February 1765 William Hutton noted his own reluctance to travel to Moseley to collect the payment for a book and in the 1767 Turnpike Trust Act the route was described as "narrow, incommodious and dangerous to travellers in several places". The new Turnpike Road to Alcester solved the problem although the Trust charged tolls to recoup its expenditure. The absence of the traditional squire of long established family may also have attracted these often self-made men, conscious of their own considerable achievements. Not all the Moseley Hall estate had been bought by the Taylors. Other purchasers were Stephen Breford, George Dalloway, James Payton, John and William Russel and Roger Vaughton.

A few wills and inventories are available for the eighteenth and early nineteenth centuries. Benjamin and his quarrelsome family had humbler relatives to watch their downfall. A Benjamin Grevis who died in 1700 described himself as "gentleman" but left all his goods to his brother James "yeoman of Moseley". They were worth £113.3.5 and included the usual crops, stock and equipment but also books and a looking-glass. William Bryan, a yeoman who died in 1738, was much more prosperous and his inventory reached a value of £369.4.2. His house was not large but neighbours owed him £100 in cash and bonds. Husbandman Richard Briscoe's goods in 1723 were worth £38.15.0. and he signed his will with a mark. All three evidently made their own cheese and both Grevis and Bryan brewed.

The name of Marston first occurs in the will of Thomas, who died in 1545, and appears next in that of Helen in 1605. The spinster Anne who died in 1767 was evidently wealthy although she just made her mark. She was probably the donor of the communion service presented to Moseley Chapel in 1759. She asked to be buried in a lead coffin under the communion table and left 10/6 a year for a sermon and divine service to be provided there on Good Friday for the forty years succeeding her death. The same sum was to be spent annually on bread and alms for poor women but these must be "proper, honest, industrious and deserving". A note attached to the will explains that Ann's land was in plots among that of a Mr. Withers, presumably Charles Trubshaw Withers of Wake Green, and that he hoped to buy it as soon as her estate was wound up, though "a Mr. Taylor" was also interested.

A yeoman William Marston died in 1773 and the 1794 will of one William Fisher of Moseley mentions a son-in-law, Samuel Marston of Garretts Green. Fisher's possessions included a silver watch and china, a lately acquired farm at Five Ways and land leased from Dr. Smallbrook. His executor lived in West Heath.

There are no Rotton wills for the eighteenth century and the name does not occur in the Moseley Registers, available for baptisms from 1758 and burials from 1762. In 1696 Stratford Place and its fields were conveyed to the trustees of William Simcox, a West Bromwich yeoman, by Thomas Rotton and his mortgagees, which suggests that mismanagement or misfortune may have struck the family. Evidently the name does not recur in the Birmingham area except in the unfortunately named bank "Rotton and Onions" which existed early in the nineteenth century.

There may be traces of the Beddyl family in register entries for Beddells in 1848 and Biddles in 1763, 1767, 1781 and 1784. Entries for Watton end with the funeral of William in March 1807. The ancient Moseley families must have been dying out or moving on as the influx began of men involved in Birmingham industry.

Many of the newcomers stayed a very short time. If probable spelling errors are eliminated, it is found that 112 names occur only once in the registers for the period 1761-1799. Of course marriages were not included.

The names of some inhabitants become familiar on a variety of other legal documents, notices and also advertisements in "Aris' Gazette". Mr. George Cotton caused consternation when in 1766 he bought from one Richard Hiles the lease granted by the churchwardens of land reserved for the maintenance of the Kings Norton poor. He erected two buildings instead of the one they had approved, used two acres for a timber yard and sub-let a meadow and Cottage to William Anderton. Bentley's Directory of 1841 lists a descendant of the same name and trade and Cotton Lane perpetuates their memory today. He must have been interested in offers such as the two hundred oaks and fifty-four ash trees advertised by the Widow Cotterell in 1761.

The Swan Inn on the Alcester Road, almost opposite the modern Chantry Road, was rented by John Strettill from 1763 onwards. With the building went gardens, a pasture and meadows. In 1777 he lost "a brown and white young fox hound dog" for whom he offered a reward of 5/-. In the 1780s he opened the Moseley Nursery which still existed in 1801.

Thomas Blakemore was the licensee of the Bull's Head. He had land of his own, sold in 1770, and evidently acted as an agent because in 1768 the advertisement of a Yardley property advised that he would show the premises and he was listed as paying in another's rates for the 1787 Poor Relief Assessment. He had problems, however, because in 1781 he publicly repudiated all his wife's future debts by a notice in "Aris' Gazette". In 1791 the Bull's Head and seven adjoining tenements were let for £41 .9.0. Presumably both he and Strettill brewed their own beer like the licensee of the Fox and Dogs, later the Fighting Cocks, whose brewing equipment was advertised for sale in 1774.

Then there was Charles Trubshaw Withers, who had been mayor of Worcester in 1758. He was allocated land to enclose in 1774 on Kings Heath, adjacent to Wake Green, for which he was charged surveyors' fees of £22.7.3., and he died in 1804.

In 1772 an anonymous resident of Moseley published "Truth and Recreation obtained in Land Surveying and Mensuration or the Description and Use of Instruments and Propositions to that end intended by the Author". No evidence of its success is available.

Mr. Thomas Lakin Hawkes had other problems when in February 1790 it was necessary for Mr. John Lane of Wake Green to advertise that the report that he had described Mr. Hawkes as "disaffected to Government" was "a gross calumny and destitute of the smallest foundation whatever in truth". Was he perhaps a descendant of the John and Katherine Hawkis who joined the Guild of St. Anne in 1492? Perhaps he and Mr. Lane consulted Thomas Aris Pearson, sole proprietor of "Aris' Gazette", who lived at Moor Green until his death in 1801.

In the second half of the eighteenth century Moseley began its long association with private education. The only grammar school for Moseley boys would be that of Kings Norton. There is no way of knowing now who were the pupils of the private schools established in Moseley but possibly boarders came from Birmingham to enjoy the healthy village air and local boys may have joined them during the week at least.

In 1767 Mr. and Mrs. Halford advertised their Boarding School at Wake Green. Admission cost 5/-; board, writing and arithmetic were 10 guineas a year and reading and needlework, presumably for girls, were an extra eight guineas. In 1769 Miss Henrietta Johnson from Hereford advertised that she would "open a boarding school on Monday, 22nd May for the reception of young ladies at the late house of Mr. Bedford, near Moseley . . . pleasantly situated on Cannon Hill." She extolled its "very fine, healthful Air" and continued that "they who please to favour her with the education of their children may depend on having them treated with the greatest care and tenderness and the utmost pain taken to improve their morals in virtue and every genteel accomplishment". In

1787 "W. Lander, late writing and drawing master at the Free School Birmingham" advertised an Academy near the Chapel by the Turnpike Road where young gentlemen would be "genteely boarded, tenderly treated and carefully instructed in every branch of useful and polite education necessary to form the scholar and man of business", including "such branches of Science as may have a reference to their intended Trades or Professions"-all for £15 pa. with washing, though Latin and Drawing were 10/6 extra a quarter. He was already interested in attracting the sons of local industrialists and business men. Finally the Reverend John Hobson, a Presbyterian Minister, opened a school on Balsall Heath but this house was burnt down during the Priestley Riots of 1791.

There is some evidence of how well-to-do inhabitants spent their time. Certain men would undertake the duties connected with care of the poor or sit as Justices of the Peace in the Magistrates' Courts, which were evidently held at the Fighting Cocks or Fox and Dogs when justice was required in this area. They may have gone to local events such as waggoner George Guest setting out from Wake Green to walk 1,000 miles in twenty-eight days for a bet, or the Main of Cocks held at the Fighting Cocks on December 26th, 1759, between the gentlemen of Worcestershire and Warwickshire, when fifteen cocks either side battled for two guineas a contest or £10 the main. Especially after the turnpike road was made they would have had the opportunity of joining in contemporary Birmingham's very active cultural life. Privileged men might have been invited to the meetings of the Lunar Society or have joined the Birmingham Library or have attended the Triennial Music Festivals in aid of the General Hospital, the literary discussions in Freeth's Tavern, plays in one of the three theatres or the regular assemblies. Perhaps they patronised the Moseley Theatre, built entirely of wood in 1777 on the Alcester Road in the parish of Aston. "Henry Ill" and a musical entertainment called "The Waterman" were performed there in late July and "The Beggar's Opera" in August 1777. Boxes cost 3/-, pit 2/-, and gallery 1/-. Unfortunately the building was burnt to the ground in 1778.

They must also have been interested in building because Spurrier in 1908 listed as constructed at this time the two Moseley Halls, the Andertons' Mansion House in the modern Belle Walk area, Woodfield nearby, Kingswood where a road so named is now and Highfield House, still standing at the top of Church Road. In addition were Green Hill House and the Mounts, Hern Hill and the Leasowes along Wake Green Road. Moseley House was built opposite Moseley Chapel in what is now St. Mary's Row, and Sansome's School was probably the red brick building at the corner of Church Road (then known as Ladypool Lane) and what was to become Blaney Street or Woodbridge Road. Another late eighteenth century house stands in the latter road overlooking the later railway line and others were built between it and what was to become Trafalgar Road. Even if Spurrier was wrong to assume that all these were late eighteenth century rather than early nineteenth, they were certainly in the simple Georgian style and must have contrasted pleasantly with the remaining half-timbered structures.

An unnamed house offered for sale in 1781 was described as having two front parlours, a small sitting room, five chambers, garrets, kitchen, brewhouse, cellars, stables and gardens. Perhaps the quality of furnishings is suggested by the sale catalogue for the contents of Thomas Aris Pearson's House, sold in February 1802 but presumably in use in the late eighteenth century. His four mahogany fourposter beds were curtained with white dimity and yellow and green moreen and contained "superfine seasoned goose and down feather" mattresses.

The number of small businesses had increased with the population. As well as obvious places such as the smithy there were a bleach yard and thread works advertised to let in 1789, and the tannery listed in the 1787 Poor Relief Assessment. The mills at Moor Green and Sarehole were still in use.

In 1772 the Enclosure Act for the Parish of Kings Norton was passed and the allocation of common land was made to "the owners and proprietors of lands and tenements within and parcel of the said manor" in 1774. It is believed that only a strip with an average width of 180 yards on either side of the Turnpike Road on Balsall Heath and Kings Heath and the very small areas of Moor Green and Wake Green were left unenclosed by this date and various lists of fines exist which were charged for encroachment on the waste of Kings Norton manor during the seventeenth and eighteenth Centuries. A map made about 1770 *(as seen on page on 18)* bears out this supposition as, except for those areas and Moseley Hall Park, what is known as Moseley today seems to have been divided in fields by that date. Unfortunately copies of the map which should have accompanied the allocation of 1774 have disappeared and the existing text, itself an early nineteenth century copy, describes each portion in terms of the holders of those on either side of it except when it lies beside Alcester Road, Ladypool Lane, Stoney Lane or on Wake Green, Moor Green and Kings Heath.

Recipients of enclosures on Wake Green included "Edward Ferriday's heirs", John Bracebridge Hawkesford, gentleman, Joseph Healey Esq., John Lane, Sampson Lloyd, Roger Vaughton gentleman, Charles Trubshaw Withers, Esq, and "the Moseley Poor". On Moor Green land was allocated to the Reverend Richard Chambers, Richard Smallbroke and Thomas Russell, and on Balsall Heath to Vincent Edwards, Thomas Peach and Ann Tucker, Joseph Radford, Thomas Russell, Ann Sawyer and James Taylor. According to the Rate Book of 1782 there were only twelve occupiers of houses or lands on Balsall Heath at that date. Land was also allocated to Trustees, for the Minister of Moseley Chapel, on Kings Heath and in the Ladypool Lane area. One sixteenth of the waste was the King's share.

Careful provision was made for roads: Alcester Turnpike Road, Edgbaston Lane which was designated a public road and highway, a road across Wake Green to Yardley, Moor Green Road leading across Moor Green to Kings Norton and various "drift roads".

Charges for enclosure were allocated in proportion to the size of the award. Thomas Russell was most heavily assessed at £27.5.5, then John Taylor Esq. at £26.60. Mr John Taylor was charged £1.5.9., the lowest fee of all.

As so little land in Moseley remained to be enclosed by 1772 it seems unlikely that the poor suffered as much as in other areas where they were still benefitting from squatters' cottages and the chance to use pasture and woodland resources freely. Yet as the local community had developed in the late eighteenth century the poor had certainly become an increasingly serious problem. The Poor Law of 1601 had made all parishes responsible for any who became dependent on charity. The 1662 Act of Settlement had authorised parish authorities to expel any newcomer unable to provide security within forty days and in 1722 the Workhouse Act enabled parishes to build workhouses and to refuse relief to all who refused to enter them.

In 1701 Job Marston of Hall Green had bequeathed £100 to buy land of which the Chaplain of Moseley was to enjoy the profits, or, failing such a person, the poor. This afterthought suggests that the latter were not then an obvious problem. Yet, in 1747 John Hillier left 20/- a year to the poor of Moseley. In 1778 a re-assessment of the Poor Rate was necessary and in 1787 "the growing evil of the poor" was reported in "Aris' Gazette" as the parish authorities were no longer willing to pay rents for them.

Eighteenth century assessments of Poor Rate for Moseley Yield which still exist show that the rate 'for the necessary relief of old, impotent, blind and other poor" was 2d. in the £. in the year May 1787 to April 1788 and also from 1788 to 1789. In the years 1789 to 1790 and 1798 to 1799 it was 6d. in the £.

Payments were listed in two categories, monthly and necessity. Records for the years 1774 to 1782 and 1789 to 1800 are available in Birmingham Reference Library. Overseers of the poor varied in the amount of detail which they recorded but monthly payments were obviously made to those in chronic need such as widows, the disabled and the fatherless, so they varied little in the course of any one year. In the period 1774-1782 the highest monthly outlay necessary was £9.11.0. in May 1780, whereas it was often over £20 in the period 1789 to 1800 and reached a peak of £23. in November 1796.

Widows were often paid 6/- a month although Widow Field had 8/- in 1780 and the Widow Hunt received 10/- in the same year. The allowance for illegitimate children varied from 4/- to 6/-. Other regular payments included 4/- a month to the clerk who wrote up the accounts, often with very odd spelling, and the regular purchase of parchment at three skins for 6/9d.

Necessity payments show no pattern. They were not greatest in any one month or season. The highest total in the extant records was for £49.15.9. in September 1799 but the fourth highest of £44.13.10_ was required in 1775. The variety is fascinating although it is not always possible to find examples to cover the whole period as clerks varied in style of entry so much. Clothes were provided. Men's shoes were 8/- in 1781; women's 2/- in 1789 and 3/6d in 1799; a child's 2/10 in 1791. A man's shirt, waist-coat and shoes cost 10/- in 1789; breeches cost 3/6d in 1791; shift and petticoat cost 6/-and a gown 2/- in 1794. Quality may have varied. Sometimes a boy was outfitted to go to a job: Thomas Danks received £3.3.6. for this and his journey to London in 1791.

Equipment might be needed. In 1789 William King was given a blanket at 3/6 and in 1790 a pair of bedsteads at 8/-. William Hall obtained a pair of sheets at 9/- in 1790 though another's sheets in 1798 cost only 7/8d. In 1778 half a ton of coal at 6/3 was provided and in 1794 a scythe.

Indentures for children apprenticed by the parish were comparatively expensive. In 1775 two cost 2/4d for the forms, 2/8d for inscription and 4/- for the magistrate's signature. In 1798 Benjamin Willingston's set cost 6/- altogether.

Court proceedings were costly too. In 1777 a case at the Fox and Dogs cost £1.8.11. In 1790 the examination, warrant etc. for Elizabeth Ashfield cost 4/-. In 1797 a bastardy suit cost 3/6. Officials might have to appear as in 1792 when "E. Tomkins" made three journeys to court and claimed 7/6d. Witnesses might have to travel to Worcester Sessions like Robert Cotterill on the occasion of Thomas Blakemore's case in 1781.

Poor travellers being driven from parish to parish until they reached their native one might require temporary assistance such as the 1/- given to Samuel Shakespeare because of his pass in 1790, or be taken ill in Moseley like a woman in 1789 whose care cost 4/10, or John Pennell in 1790 who was perhaps ill longer as 10/6 was needed. "Removals" may refer to such paupers who had become destitute in Moseley. In 1793 Elizabeth Avery had to be sent to Studley and in 1797 a horse was hired to carry Mary Ingram to Alvechurch.

Parishioners required aid in illness too. William Wellis was paid 7/6 when he suffered smallpox in 1778 and Mary Smith needed 4/- in 1789. Nurses might be provided or a daughter be paid an allowance for caring for her old, blind mother. In 1793 the services of a midwife cost 2/6. Possibly the elderly were given other help to keep them decent as in 1794 a women was paid 6d. to wash Joseph Cooper's shirts.

Finally came funerals. Possibly the varied prices conceal details of sex, size and rites but we do know that a child's burial cost 10/6 in 1790 whereas those of various adults cost £1.10.4 in 1778, 18/- in 1779 and £1.3.6. in 1796.

Fourteeen Moseley paupers were buried at the parish expense between 1784 and 1793.

Obviously aid was varied according to the needs of the applicant and perhaps according to the imagination of the parish overseer for Moseley Yield, who held his burdensome office for only one year, May to April. "Sixty strike of tatos for ye poor to plant" at a cost of £4.15. in May 1800 sounds like the invention born of necessity. Some families' names occur so often that it is to be hoped that the overseers were humane.

Not surprisingly crime was now sufficiently serious for "the Association in the parish of Kings Norton for the Apprehension of Felons" to be formed by 1778. In later years the members evidently enjoyed dining together but originally their purpose was more serious. One mid-eighteenth century burglar raided the house of Thomas Jacob and stole £7, seven pairs of silver cock heels, a pair of plated spurs and a flitch and a half of bacon! In 1786 another cut a panel from Mrs. Henryson's door in order to break and enter. Animals and foodstuffs must have proved a temptation to many. In 1767 a reward was offered when two sheep were killed and only the skins and heads left behind.

One of the most memorable events to take place in eighteenth century Moseley was the destruction of Moseley Hall on Saturday, 16th July, 1791, by a mob which marched from Birmingham during the Priestley Riots. There had been strong public hostility to a banquet which was held at a Birmingham hotel on July 14th, 1791, by eighty gentlemen anxious to celebrate the anniversary of the Fall of the Bastille because they supported the aims of the French Revolution. John Taylor was a Dissenter and was probably friendly with some of the group concerned, but he was neither at the banquet nor in the Birmingham area at the time. In fact he did not live at Moseley Hall but had let it to the old and blind Dowager Countess of Carhampton. According to an eye witness named John Redgrave, about two hundred people came in "huzzaing Church and King" but allowed the Countess to leave with her servants and carts full of baggage. They then feasted on livestock from the estate and set the house alight. A charming print of the subsequent scene does not suggest severe damage but Mr. Taylor claimed £3,839.5.4. before a special jury at Worcestershire Lent Assizes in March 1792. He was eventually awarded £2,700. No one was prosecuted for this particular crime though some of the rioters were tried at Worcester for other depredations.

John Standbridge of Warwick was evidently the architect of the new Moseley Hall, which was erected between 1792 and 1796, and his plans are still complete among the Taylor papers. Anyone arriving at the door would find the dining parlour and breakfast room to his right and the drawingroom at the back of the main block, with bedrooms above. Kitchens and other offices were in the right hand wing while coach house, stables, etc were in the left.

The facts that both the first and second John Taylor were absentee landowners and Dissenters and that many other prosperous residents may also have been Nonconformists probably explains why it was necessary to raise a subscription to complete the renovation of Moseley Chapel in 1782. The report in 'Aris' Gazette' stated that no service had been held there for four years. The rebuilding begun in 1780 was extensive. The "middle aisle" roof had fallen in and the new nave roof was made 7 or 8 feet higher than its predecessors as marks on the West End wall indicate. New south and north walls were built of brick, each pierced by four round headed windows. The battlements of the tower were replaced by a balluster parapet.

Moseley Hall after the Riots from a water colour made in 1791

The Reverend John Pryn Pixall LL.B., described as Vicar of Edgbaston and Curate of Moseley, may have been a worried man as he died in 1787, just after the fatal collapse of his curate Mr. Edwards in Steelhouse Lane. He received only £34 a year for his work in the village. At least he had the pleasure of receiving Anne Marston's gift of an elegant silver flagon, chalice, patten and alms dish which are still in use in St. Mary's today.

His successor was the Reverend Edward Palmer B.A. from Curdworth. He seems to have been a serious-minded, socially conscious clergyman who opened Sunday Schools where poor children might be taught to write and to read the Bible and who in 1791 initiated the tradition of an annual service at which a visiting clergyman gave an address and a collection was made for the Schools. He was appointed a chaplain to the Duchess of Cumberland in 1791 but never achieved other rank in the Church. He was disappointed in the curate's house in Moseley, possibly one of the two which were on the lych gate site, and never lived there but in one thereafter known as Parsonage or Village Green House at the corner of Oxford Road and modern St. Mary's Row. His stipend was £73 a year until 1818.

In his 1896 "Directory of Moserey" Everson referred to a now lost minute book of parish meetings held in the Bull's Head in the period 1795 to 1810. They were presided over by Mr. William Villiers, a Birmingham magistrate who lived in Moseley and had tried to save the Hall in 1791. His wife Sarah is commemorated by a plaque in the modern South Aisle which relates that she died at the Hop Pole, Worcester, while returning from Bath in 1801.

Church music was then provided by the village band. The instruments must have belonged to the parish because at one meeting the clerk's son was ordered to attend church twice every Sunday with his bassoon or to surrender it.

Moseley Hall today

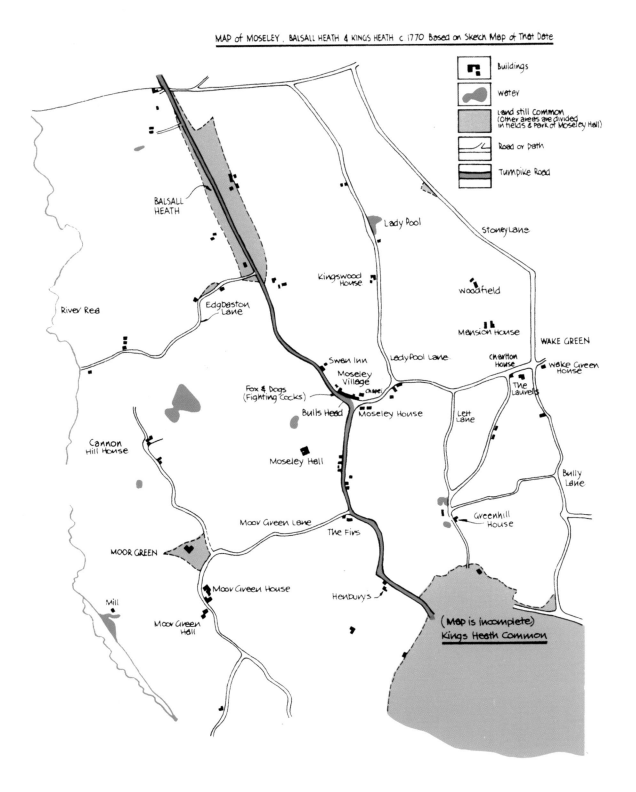

MAP of MOSELEY, BALSALL HEATH & KINGS HEATH c 1770 Based on Sketch Map of That Date

Buildings

Water

Land still Common
(Other areas are divided
in fields & park of Moseley Hall)

Road or path

Turnpike Road

BALSALL
HEATH

Lady Pool

Stoney Lane

Kingswood
House

Woodfield

River Rea

Edgbaston
Lane

Mansion House

WAKE GREEN

Swan Inn

Lady Pool Lane

Charlton
House

Wake Green
House

Moseley
Village

chapel

The
Laurels

Fox & Dogs
(Fighting Cocks)

Bulls Head

Moseley House

Left
Lane

Cannon
Hill House

Moseley Hall

Bully
Lane

Moor Green Lane

Greenhill
House

The Firs

MOOR GREEN

Mill

Moor Green House

Henburys

(Map is incomplete)
Kings Heath Common

Moor Green
Hall

CHAPTER V.

1800 - 1853
THE LAST OF RURAL LIFE

The second John Taylor must have learned to like Moseley after the new Hall was built in the 1790's, for he lived there until his death in 1814. This must have added considerable interest to village life and the social round of the local gentry. In 1804 he bought the rights of the Manor of Kings Norton from George III. His widow lived at the Hall too and then his second son James.

James Taylor was described in 1842 as having "a manly open expression of manner peculiarly striking". He was fond of business and frequently 'visited that most respectable and well constructed establishment, Messrs. Taylor and Lloyds". He was a member of the Church of England, unlike his father and grandfather, and opposed Dissenters' attempts to abolish Church rates. As a captain in the Queen's Own Worcestershire Yeomanry, he often entertained the Kings Norton troop at Moseley Hall, especially on the annual Waterloo Day when a banquet on the lawns was followed by a dance.

His son James Arthur Taylor became Conservative M.P. for East Worcestershire Parliamentary Division in 1841. He was involved in commerce and agriculture and supported his Prime Minister Sir Robert Peel on the Corn Laws, an appropriate political outlook for one whose constituents included many landowning industrialists and businessmen.

The 1843 Tithe Apportionment for the Moseley Yield indicates that at that date James Taylor of Moseley Hall was the principal landowner in Moseley with 938 acres. Then there was Isaac Anderton with 596 acres, Robert Edward Eden Mynors with 582 acres, George Attwood with 533 and W. C. Russell with 336 acres. Other landowners had much smaller estates. The Dean and Chapter of Worcester controlled the Rectorial Glebe of 316 acres and 210 acres were administered by Guardians of the Kings Norton Poor. There were over six hundred owners of land or other property listed for the area.

Farmers might be the tenants of several landowners as in the case of William Dakin who rented fields from Joseph Balden, Robert Blayney and "Moseley Chapel," or John Austin who rented from James Taylor and William Congreve Russell. Others evidently used only a small area as pasture.

James Taylor's possessions were too many to describe in words. The Anderton property lay between Stoney Lane and the site of Oakland Road, Robert Blayney's fields lay to the south of St. Mary's Row and on either side of what is now Woodbridge Road but was originally named Blayney Street after his family. William Congreve Russell, at one time M.P. for East Worcestershire, had an estate where Highbury, Pitmaston Court and Moorcroft Road are today. Russell Road is named after him. The area allocated to the Kings Norton Poor lay between Yardley Wood Road and Bully or Billesley Lane.

The field names are of some interest. "Hundreds" and "Big Hundreds Meadows" have been mentioned already as of possible Saxon origin. "Fivelands" indicates that the Open Field System did exist in Moseley at some date, because the word means a holding made up of five strips. The "Sling" by the Rea was probably land left waste between two systems of strips or as a lane. "Upper and Lower Riddings" and "The Ridding" indicate ground specially cleared and "Tinings" means a hedged enclosure. Other names indicated the locations of a marl pit, a gravel pit and a brick kiln. Several fields were named after owners, but the most intriguing are "Lions Leasow" and "Shoulder of Mutton Piece".

Bentley's Directory of 1841 listed various Moseley businesses. The Cotton family were timber merchants in the Cotton Lane area. George Johns was a builder and carpenter and William Phillips a hatter. Thomas Averill was a tailor and Thomas Maydew was the blacksmith whose forge adjoined the Bull's Head. Richard Bullock had established a business as builder and plumber which was to be the most successful in the village and the Bull's Head and Fighting Cocks were still flourishing in the charge of John Milward and Mr. and Mrs. Todd. Miss Charlotte Thru pp's boarding school lay on the south side of School Road and Hannah Sansum ran the Moseley Classical and Commercial School which had originated in a house near the Chapel.

The 1854 Post Office Directory listed thirty-three householders as "gentry". Their Houses included Moseley Hall, Moseley Grove, The Manor House, Highfield, Moseley House, Park Place, Fivelands, Henburys, Cannon Hill

House, Woodfield, Charlton Cottage, The Elms, Moor Green and The Firs.

Newcomers to trade were shopkeepers Robert Brock and James Upton, the Godso brothers, who combined building and coffin making, and Kirby and Mitchell as wheelwrights and blacksmiths. Elizabeth Boyce had opened yet another school on Wake Green and Sarah Hayes was post mistress, as the penny Post had been introduced in 1841. After 1814 the parish registers indicate that such people as whitesmiths, wire drawers and clerks were joining the exodus from Birmingham. In 1811 there were 191 households in Moseley but in 1840 the total was 380. Yet the village was still described as "pleasant and romantic", and it must have been a very healthy location. Between 1800 and 1850 ten inhabitants lived to be over 90, 44 survived into their 80's and 78 died between their seventieth and eightieth birthdays.

How did the population spend free time? In the 1820's little was formally organised. The fighting dogs match by the River Rea which led to prosecutions was probably impromptu. The lightweight boxing contest on Wake Green in 1822 was unusual enough for it to be advertised in "Aris' Gazette" with the information that Ben Preston and Bill Goold were "unknown to the ring and mere infants in Science". Probably the poorer villagers rarely used the coach which ran from the Fighting Cocks to Birmingham on Monday, Thursday and Saturday from 1815 onwards as the fare was 2/6d to ride inside. It left the village at 10 a.m. and returned at 4p.m.

The pleasant life of a prosperous gentleman farmer is described in the diary of Matthew Boulton, who lived at Wake Green between 1836 and 1841. He did record details of the agricultural year, such as bean sowing, sheep dipping, haymaking, wheat harvest, cattle sales and an exhibition of hedging and ditching, but his social life seems to have been very important to him.

He wrote poetry and declaimed it on occasions such as Queen Victoria's accession. He belonged to the Moseley Book Club which held annual dinners at the Fighting Cocks, and presumably existed for many years although its origin is unknown. He bought "The Seven Ages of England" and "A Life of Ali Pasha" there in 1837 and attended its dinners in 1839 and 1840. He accompanied Mr. Lawson the curate to a sale of books included in a Hall Green clergyman's effects.

Boulton belonged to the Queen's Own Worcestershire Yeomanry and joined them in drills on Wake Green and at the Waterloo banquets. He hunted with some trepidation. He was interested in local politics and handed out refreshment tickets at Kings Norton to those who voted for Mr. St. Paul and Mr. Barnaby in the 1837 elections. He is unlikely to have understood the aspirations of the Chartists whose Birmingham Bull Ring meeting in 1839 became so violent that the Yeomanry was summoned to assemble on Wake Green to await orders.

His life reflected the close social links with Birmingham families because he made frequent visits to their homes and dined with Mr. Cox of Temple Row on Christmas Day 1837. He bought his port wine at Smallwoods and consulted a Birmingham doctor who lived in Balsall Heath and Mr. Simcox the solicitor. He enjoyed the 1837 Music Festival where Mendelssohn's "St. Paul" was performed as well as Handel's "Messiah" and visited the great Whit Fair. He also belonged to the Birmingham Society for Natural History.

Although used to travel, including holidays in North Wales, the centre of Boulton's world was Moseley because he inherited the property there of his relative Joseph Dyott of Wake Green. He was concerned with the affairs of Moseley Chapel and recorded impressions of sermons and of a vestry meeting about the renovation of the tower as well as the marriages and funerals of neighbours. In the North aisle hangs a plaque which commemorates his sadly early death from pleurisy in 1841.

If Matthew Boulton had lived to old age he would have seen a very different Moseley develop. The change began on Balsall Heath when in 1828 it was agreed by the mortgagees of the Frowd and Moore estate to lay out roads, including Balsall Heath Road, to link the Alcester Trunk Road and Pershore Road. Birmingham men were interested in building cheap housing for their rapidly increasing work force. In 1833 the Reverend Vincent Edwards, a Nonconformist minister, sold his land between the River Rea and Alcester Road so Vincent, Tindal, George and Wenman Streets were soon marked out and lined by small, closely packed houses. In 1835 building activity intensified in the area between Alcester Road and Ladypool Lane. In 1838 the Haden estate, named after a buttonmaker who had built a house there in 1791, was sold for the development of Belgrave and Haden Streets. By that year the population of the Heath justified the erection of a Wesleyan Chapel in Vincent Street. The area was within the Manor of Kings Norton and inhabitants were supposed to worship at Moseley Chapel but probably many were Nonconformist and their links were with Birmingham life. The 1840 Tithe Map shows a network of narrow streets developing between the Alcester Turnpike and Mary Street although Everson wrote in 1896 that blackberries and nuts grew by Balsall Heath Road and the Rea was still a sparkling stream where pike and crayfish might be caught as late as 1850.

Public health was to become a very serious problem and typhoid epidemics spread from Balsall Heath to more salubrious Moseley. In 1858 the Balsall Heath Sanitary Board was established and become an energetic organ of local government. Town life had not yet reached Moseley, though its own population was 1,900 in 1850, but change was to be very rapid in the second half of the nineteenth century.

Many social problems were growing with the population. In 1834 the Poor Law Amendment Act was passed which authorised the formation of unions of parishes to build workhouses so that the poor might be encouraged to become self-supporting by the application of the less eligibility principle which made any relief less tolerable than the most humble independence. Only those who were not able-bodied were entitled to any other form of relief than as inmates of the dreaded workhouse.

Unfortunately the records for Kings Norton Union are lost except for the Relieving Officer's Application Book for June 1849. Balsall Heath applicants included Benjamin Child, a tube maker of 28, Robert Brownall, a grinder aged 43, and Joseph Hemming of the same trade who had six children but suffered from consumption. Moseley applicants included Joseph Kimberley, cordwainer, and William Tranter, nailer, whose weekly incomes were 12/- and 10/- respectively. Some were disabled by ill-health but others asked help in particular emergencies such as children's illnesses. Presumably such crises were often the last straw. William Tranter asked help when a son was ill and received meal and 1/7½d, but when he returned because his wife had fallen sick too he was ordered to the workhouse. At sixty-five years old he may have had little hope of ever obtaining work again. Widows featured frequently in the records: Rebecca Shipston was a washerwomen who required temporary assistance and received 4/- worth of provisions. Obedience Bayliss, aged 86, asked only for a pair of shoes but then she was in regular receipt of 2/- and a loaf each week. Elizabeth Tomkins was single but had three children. Her income as a washerwomen was 5/- a week and she obtained a medical note. Mary Ann Davis asked only for shoes and stockings as she was going into service. The poor were numerous enough for a surgeon to be oppointed for Moseley Yield in 1835.

The homes of more prosperous Moseley residents were still very tempting to criminals. In 1828 Richard Mavis and Ebenezer Collins were sentenced to two months hard labour for breaking down James Taylor's garden fence. By 1838 there was anxiety over frequent burglaries of wine cellars and in 1852 the Lime Grove house of Mr. Tarleton was robbed of £40 worth of silver. The Kings Norton Association for the Apprehension of Felons still existed and probably helped to arrange the appointment of a horse patrol in 1838 and of two policemen for Wake Green in 1850.

The most exciting events in the first half of the nineteenth century must have been Queen Victoria's Coronation Celebrations and the opening of the Birmingham Gloucester Railway. The Coronation was celebrated by the whole Community. The National School pupils and poor adults were feasted in booths. The Queen's Own Regiment of Worcestershire Yeomanry "assembled on Wake Green, fired three rounds, drank her Majesty's health and expressed their attachment with three times three hearty cheers" "after which they were refreshed with a substantial breakfast in the good old English style (provided) by their two lieutenants and cornet". James Taylor of the Hall was presented to the young monarch at a royal levée the following month, so details of her appearance and manner would soon be common knowledge locally.

In 1836 Parliament passed an act permitting the Birmingham and Gloucester Railway Company to lay a line through Balsall Heath and to the East of Moseley Chapel. Local people were quick to see the advantages of such speedy transport to Birmingham, but seized the chance of compensation for land required, as at the Fighting Cocks meeting held in 1837 to discuss the future Brighton Road bridge site. Now not only those who kept carriages could live in Moseley, and after 1833 many small houses were to be built even on the sites of proud mansions. Unfortunately there seem to be no local records of the impression which the construction of the railway made, but it is easy to imagine the endless discussions on its likely consequences and the many walks to view the cutting, the navvies at work and eventually the first trains. Six men died in accidents while working on the track in the parish in 1840. The original Moseley Station was near the modern Kings Heath Library site.

Life at Moseley Chapel did not stand still. In 1806 a barrel organ was obtained which played eight or nine hymn tunes and was perched in a loft, entered from the belfry. After fifteen years the Cole family band was hired for three

St. Mary's the Rickman nave with later additions

months but proved too expensive. Mr. Cole and his four sons played a violin, oboe, clarinet, bass and double bass.

In 1823 it was necessary to enlarge the Chapel. Two thousand pounds were raised by voluntary subscriptions and Thomas Rickman, a Birmingham pioneer of the Gothic Revival, was engaged as architect. The nave was rebuilt and the roof was raised to span the whole church. The brick walls were plastered within and without to resemble stone, and the flat ceiling was crossed by parallel and diagonal imitation oak beams and plaster. Cast iron tracery was added to the windows and a gallery was built at the West End. There was no chancel so the altar stood in a semi-circular recess, the ceiling of which was painted sky blue sprinkled with gilt stars. Miss Sarah Taylor gave a new barrel organ which played thirty tunes on three barrels. Wind was supplied to it by a foot treadle. The box pews were high walled and lit by candles for the occasional evening service. Three hundred and sixty free "sittings" were provided for the poor, thanks to the generosity of a few individuals and the contribution of the Society for Enlarging Churches and Chapels. The re-building cost also the life of David Archer, a mason from Perth in Scotland.

On 17th March, 1824, the Bishop of Worcester consecrated the renovated Chapel and a new burial ground in the presence of a congregation described as "large and highly respectable". The anthems for the occasion were performed by the Birmingham Oratorio Society and the collection totalled £106.0.9. His Lordship then partook of a collation at the curate's home.

By the end of 1824, the Reverend Edward Palmer was so ill that he issued a printed exhortation to his congregation on New Year's Day 1825. In 1826 he died aged 72 years and was described in "Aris' Gazette" as "a lover of all them who love our Lord Jesus Christ in sincerity". Joseph Bissell, his former clerk, died in 1827 at the great age of 98. He had served the Chapel for forty years.

Mr. Palmer's successor was the Reverend Walter Farquhar Hook, whose character is vividly revealed in letters to his mother, which were preserved when he became the eminent Dean of Chichester. He described Moseley on his arrival as "just the place where I can live and die in peace and seclusion, which is all I want. We have a capital shop in the village where meat and beer, cheese and eggs and whipcord and thread, tops and ginger bread and garden stuff and bread and milk and cream and almost everything are sold". His stipend was £150 p.a. so he drank raspberry vinegar, rather than wine, and ate beef and mutton as he was anxious to spend liberally in the parish.

The young curate was active in Birmingham, where he became Lecturer of St. Philip's Church, and made snap judgements such as that a certain Bishop's Chaplain and his wife were "as full of spiritual pride as an egg is of meat". He was anxious to combat Nonconformist influences and referred to the extreme Evangelicals as "Saints". Unfortunately we do not know if he attended the meeting held at the Fighting Cocks in January 1829 to oppose the Catholic Emancipation Bill.

His concern for the poor may have been stimulated by the discovery that they never carried their dead into the Chapel, as the previous curate had charged a hat band or half a guinea for the privilege. Hook insisted on funerals being held inside the building. He also determined to open a school where such people might obtain a basic education. He wrote to his mother "what with computing the expense, talking over my neighbours, preaching two sermons to convince the rich of the necessity of establishing schools, drawing up resolutions, superintend mg the plans and estimates of builders, applying to everyone who thinks himself a gentleman and soliciting his support, I am pretty busy". A committee was formed by himself. James Taylor of Moseley Hall, Isaac Anderton, Thomas Salmon and William C. Russell. Mr. Taylor gave a 99 years lease of a quarter acre in Lett Lane at a rent of one guinea p.a. and the school building was erected for £465.

At Midsummer 1827 the Sunday Schools were discontinued and the money in hand was paid to the treasurer of the new National School. On Easter Day 1828 it was opened. A procession of ninety-seven boys and eighty-two girls marched to the Chapel to hear a sermon by the curate, then they were "regaled in the School with a dinner of Roast Beef and Plumb Pudding". Rules were strict. Pupils had to attend school on week-days and twice on Sundays to accompany the Master and Mistress to the Chapel. Repeated absences led to expulsion, and personal appearance was important: pupils must be "clean washed and combed with their hair cut short and their clothes well mended. The girls to wear no curls or combs". Parents were to pay 2d a week per child which was to be spent on clothing for the pupils. They were expected to go into domestic service eventually. Evidently there was considerable absenteeism and some parents had the temerity to oppose the rules, but the school developed healthily and steadily.

The first Master and Mistress were Henry Harris and his wife who received a joint salary of fifty guineas a year and the use of a house. Presumably they taught by the monitorial system adopted in the Anglican National Society Schools, which required the teacher to impart each lesson in turn to the brightest pupils, each of whom then repeated it to about ten others who were younger or less able. According to the first annual report in 1830, only the "3 R's" were taught but error must have been common.

Unfortunately Mr. Hook was too well connected to stay long in Moseley, still an insignificant though pleasant place. He became Vicar of Trinity Church, Coventry, and was succeeded in 1831 by the Reverend William Morrell Lawson, M.A.

Mr. Lawson was a Yorkshire man. Mrs. Underhill of "Hayfield" built "The Vale" opposite her own house as a parsonage for him and he stayed until ill-health caused his resignation in 1852. Little is known of his curacy but Matthew Boulton wrote of his "eloquent and forceful language" and enjoyed his company. He continued the custom of inviting well known clergymen to preach the annual sermon in aid of the Chapel's schools.

In 1853 Moseley became a District Chapelry by an Order in Council of Queen Victoria. The boundary lay along the limits of Northfield and Edgbaston parishes to the West, up Edgbaston Lane, southwards along the Alcester Road, up Trafalgar Road and eastwards towards Stoney Lane, along that Lane to Wake Green Road, from there to Sarehole and then to Haunch Lane and. Alcester Lane's End. Now baptisms, churchings, marriages and burials might not only be performed there by the curate but also he might keep the fees. It was not until 1866 that the District became a separate parish, independent of Kings Norton and Bromsg rove, with the title of Vicar to offer its incumbent. In 1854 a red brick vicarage was built in School Lane.

In 1853 Balsall Heath was also separated from Kings Norton Parish and from the official care of the Moseley clergy as the new church of St. Paul's was built. The boundaries of this District Chapelry lay along Edgbaston Lane, the east bank of the Rea, Belgrave Road, Stoney Lane and Brighton Road. The foundation stone was laid by Mrs. James Taylor of Moseley Hall, where the party of clergy and local worthies assembled to attend a service in Moseley Chapel and then go down the Alcester Road to the site in procession with "charity and National School children," the responsible committee, the architect, builder and friends." The population of Balsall Heath was stated to be between 3,000 and 4,000 and it was emphasised that the distance from Moseley had obliged the few affluent families to employ their servants and horses on the Sabbath, contrary to scriptural precept, and made the respectable tradesmen's houses "undesirable". In fact St. Paul's was a very fashionable church for some years. Balsall Heath was now recognised as distinct from Moseley and in 1891 it became part of Birmingham. Its boundary with Moseley lay along Edgbaston and Brighton Roads.

CHAPTER VI.

MOSELEY 1853 - 1914
SOCIAL SUMMIT

After the death of James Taylor in 1852 the Hall was occupied only by servants until William Dawes and his family rented it.

In 1884 Richard Cadbury, the benevolent Quaker chocolate manufacturer, became the tenant. It must have affected village life that he was a Nonconformist and one can image the talk when in 1888 officials visited the Hall to levy a distraint for tithes. He gave hospitality to local events such as the Horticultural Show of 1884 but also to a temperance conference and to tramway servants, invited to breakfast in 1889. Old people at an 1890 party were entertained by the Bournville band. In 1890 Richard Cadbury bought the Hall from the Taylor Estate and in 1891 presented it to Birmingham Town Council to become Moseley Hall Convalescent Hospital for Children. He himself moved to Uffculme and eventually died in Jerusalem in 1899.

The new hospital must have seemed wonderful to the children, many from very poor Birmingham homes, who recovered there. The wards were gradually furnished with comforts given often by Moseley residents, including Sunday School children, and the grounds were extensive and beautifully landscaped. An article written in 1894 refers to one child gaining 9 lbs in weight in a month there, while another gained 15 lbs in seven weeks. The sum of 3/4½d a week was thought adequate to support either a patient or a member of staff.

At Christmas local people gathered toys, especially at St. Mary's Toy Service, and these were distributed by Father Christmas and attendant "fairies" during the course of a special tea party. From 1895 until the First World War an annual Bicycle Gymkhana was held in the Hall park to raise funds. This has been described by those who enjoyed it as children as the occasion on which everyone in Moseley united. There were races which involved potato spearing, needle-threading and cycling in couples and a prize was presented for the most beautifully decorated bicycle. In 1898 this was awarded to one of which the frame was covered with pines, pyretherum and white ribbon, the back wheel with comflowers and blue ribbon and the front with geraniums and red ribbon. On the handlebars was a bouquet of red poppies, blue lupins and white gladioli, tied with red, white and blue ribbon. So much for Moseley taste at that date.

The owners of other large houses were to take the lead in community life in turn. The Sneyd-Kynnersleys of Moor Green Hall were very active at St. Mary's. Mr. T. C. Sneyd-Kynnersley who died in 1892 was Stipendiary of Birmingham for 35 years. In 1860 Moor Green Cottage became known as Pitmaston and in 1884 was sold to John Holder, a Birmingham brewer who owned a music hall in Park Street. He and his family worked with Canon Colmore in Moseley, but he was prominent in Birmingham too, especially as Chairman of the General Hospital at the end of the Century, and he was knighted in 1898.

The Chamberlain family lived in the area although they do not seem to have played a significant part in the community, not only it would seem because their activities were based in Birmingham or London, but also because they were Nonconformist. Joseph Chamberlain lived at Highbury from 1881 until his death. The house was described in Everson's 1896 Directory as being built in brick with stone facings in the "modern Gothic" style and the electric lighting, conservatories and orchid houses were thought worthy of special note. Arthur Chamberlain lived at Moor Green Hall. Austen Chamberlain became M.P. for the constituency of East Worcestershire,. in which Moseley lay, in 1892. Various horticultural shows and other events were held at their homes and "The Birmingham and Moseley Society Journal", which was to be printed under various titles from 1892 until 1933, recorded all the honours the family achieved as well as occasions such as Joseph's homecoming with his third bride in 1888.

Other prominent men, like John Holder and the Chamberlains, were also involved in local industry or trade. James Smith of the Dingle, now Gracie Hall on Wake Green Road, was an iron bedstead maker who was last Mayor of Birmingham in 1895 and first Lord Mayor in 1896. In 1899 he moved to Edgbaston Hall. John Padmore of the Grange, Wake Green Road, was a gold refiner and John Skinner had a well known and still surviving boot and shoe shop in Broad Street, Birmingham. Business success and consequent wealth were much respected although occasionally the editor of "The Moseley Society Journal" expressed himself oddly as in the biography of Mr. Alfred Heath "whose training commenced at a very early age and he blossomed forth into a full blown manufacturer before most boys have given up kites and catapults". There was also respect for less exalted but very real achievement. Other biographies were of Mr. James Bullock, whose family had a long established building business, and W. J. Davies, General Secretary of the Amalgamated Society of Brassworkers who lived in Trafalgar Road.

Society was carefully graded and each group lived in a recognised area. The most successful and wealthy occupied houses such as Pitmaston, Moor Green Hall and Highbury. Then there were the families who lived in large grounds on the Wake Green Road where there was plenty of room for stables and coach-houses. The residents of Chantry Road and Park Hill were very prosperous but mostly unlikely to vie with Wake Green Road, and then there were the smaller villas which were built as the big houses were demolished when heads of families like the Andertons and Taylors died and their heirs sold the land once farmed. In Moseley village itself were the homes of shopkeepers and small craftsmen, some labourers and eventually men such as clerks who could afford small terraced houses in Farquhar and Tudor Roads.

**The Mansion House
Anderton Park
from a nineteenth century print**

Several maps of parts of nineteenth century Moseley still exist, many made in connection with sales of land for building and so covering only a small area. There are also the Tithe Map of 1840 and Ordnance Survey of 1888, so the progress of building can be checked at varied if arbitrary intervals.

In 1840 Moseley Village was the curved row of buildings from the Bull's Head to the Church, opposite which stood only Moseley House. There were a few big houses between the village and Balsall Heath along the eastern side of Alcester Road and along Wake Green Road, but on the western side of the former Turnpike Road lay Moseley Hall Park from the Reddings to Park Road. Between it and the Rea stood a few more big houses such as Moor Green. Farms surrounded the area on Kings Heath, beyond Billesley Lane and between the Andertons' mansion and Balsall Heath.

In 1858 the area between School Lane, Valentine Road, the railway line and the parsonage grounds, was being built up. Moseley station lay on the east side of the Alcester Road, opposite Valentine Road.

In 1865 Park Hill was laid out and the ancient footpath from Alcester Road to Edgbaston Lane was closed. In 1868 Blayney Street was named and St. Mary's Row recognised although shops and houses were not built opposite the church until after 1878.

In 1870 a triangle of land bounded by Greenhill Road, Cotton Lane and the future Oxford Road was sold in small lots for villas.

In 1872 the toil gate at the top of Park Hill was demolished. Public opinion no longer approved of Turnpike Trusts and Parliament refused to pass Continuation Acts, as adequate profits had been made.

In 1877 the Anderton Park Estate was sold and many new houses were built in the eastern sections of Forest Road, Woodstock Road, all Sandford Road and Belle Walk. The map also indicates on the western side of Wake Green Road "The Laurels" between Billesley and Cotton Lanes, "Ivythorpe" which must have preceded "The Dingle," "The Grove" on the site of Grove Avenue and "The Elms" on the site of the Meteor Garage. Kingswood House and Highfield House still stood and there were a few big houses in Church, Oakland and Forest Roads. Trafalgar Road was mostly built up though described as new in the 1853 Order in Council, with a skating rink near the Trafalgar Hotel, and so was the south side of Woodbridge Road. There were no longer vacant lots between Trafalgar Road and Moseley Village though Moseley Hall Park still stretched on the west side of the main road. Moseley Station was on its present site off Blayney Street, renamed Wood bridge Road because of the wooden structure which spanned the railway line until 1894.

By 1888 more houses lined Wake Green Road, Oxford Road had been laid from the village as far as School Road and Ascot Road was built. Church Road and the area between it and Trafalgar Road were covered with houses. Yet there were still two farms in the triangle formed by Woodstock Road, Stoney Lane and Ladypool Lane, as well as Coldbath and Billesley Farms in "Moseley in Yardley" and Moorcroft and Moor Green Farms between Moseley Park and the River Rea. The great Cannon Hill and Calthorpe Parks lay between these and Edward Road, where the densely populated areas of Balsall Heath began. Only a few houses stood together in a block in Russell Road, which was used by the residents of Pitmaston. This mansion was on the site of the Ideal Benefit Society head offices. Hill House and Hill Crest must have stood on the edge of the park. At an unknown date between 1840 and 1888 the Prince of Wales was built because it appears on the Ordinance Survey Map of the latter date and not on the Tithe Map.

By 1889 Strensham Road and Augusta Road were built up and the occupiers were able to buy their sites from the Taylor Estate. Chantry Road was laid out in the early 1890's. In 1895 Farquhar and Tudor Roads were rising and in 1896 workmen began to cut Salisbury Road through the Hall Park. This was named after the contemporary Prime Minister. Everson's Directory lists forty-six roads in the polling district of Moseley.

It is noticeable that a very high proportion of the houses have names not numbers. "The Moseley & Kings Heath Journal" advertised the latest furniture and household equipment. Its gardening correspondent advised dahlias, lobelias, sweet peas, asters, herbaceous, calceolarias, pelargoniums and gladioli for "villa gardens".

Many buildings which might have been interesting were demolished. Richard Cadbury pulled down the Henburys in 1895 and added its grounds to Uffculme. There may have been a house on that site since the late medieval period. Moseley House, occupied in the nineteenth century by a Mr. Cohen and then by a maltster named Gomm, disappeared in 1878. Bank House, latterly a respected school, the Warren, Woodfield and Kingswood followed in the 1890's. Even Moseley Village had lost the rural appearance shown in an oil painting of perhaps a decade earlier.

Shop fronts must have lined the east side of the main road and the Fighting Cocks, rebuilt in 1899, was rather ugly. In 1900 there was a public outcry when the Hall Lodge was demolished and Victoria Parade replaced not only it, but also a rookery in tall elms and a fragrant bluebell wood which a public fund failed to save. In 1894 there were criticisms of the wooden pavements in the main shopping area and in 1897 these were asphalted by the Kings Norton Rural District Council.

Everson lists the shopkeepers and tradesmen of 1896 who included W. S. Brassington, an amateur historian and chemist, as well as Mr. Lowther the other chemist. Thomas Luker, the Woodbridge Road baker, and Mathias Watts, the art dealer and picture framer, had surnames which still decorate shop fronts in 1973. There were two bakers, two butchers, two grocers, one poulterer, one fruiterer, a bookseller and a newsagent. Fashion was represented by two boot-makers, Mr. Noon the tailor, a milliner, a dressmaker and a hairdresser. There were two plumbers, a builder and a housepainter, dealers in furniture, ironmongery and coal, a watchmaker, and the proprietors of a cab firm and "The Village Coffee House". In 1883 Lloyds Bank had opened a Moseley branch and in 1900 a new post office was housed in the red brick Victoria Parade.

A further list exists for 1901, when Cornish Brothers had opened a Library in Moseley Village. In 1905 Motor Works were opened near the Post office; in 1907 Mr. Simpson was established as a hairdresser in St Mary's Row and in 1912 the Spring Hill firm of Gascoignes opened a shop in the same street. Moseley was now quite like its modern namesake. Yet in 1901 it was possible to write "Those who have come to regard Moseley as almost a small town were rather surprised the other day to learn that a fox had come to a finish within sound of the parish church bells". It was no longer the 1870 area of "villas and rural retreats" but supplied with gas lighting in 1877 and electricity at the end of the century.

There were still many private schools including Moseley Ladies College in The Vale, Hildathorpe in Park Hill for girls; Lonsdale House and Woodroughs for boys; Moseley Modern School in School Road, Kingsley House in Coppice Road and Aubyn House at the corner of Trafalgar and Alcester Roads.

Most Moseley people must now have travelled frequently to Birmingham, many men to work and all to enjoy the shops, theatres, etc. for which "The Moseley & Kings Heath Journal" carried so many advertisements. An omnibus covered the journey ten times a day from 1859 onwards and in 1887 lines for steam trams were laid through the Village, although this caused the formation of the Anti-Steam Tram Nuisance Society lead by the Vicar.

The open country was disappearing rapidly but fortunately local people had been very generous in providing parks. In 1873 Miss Ryland gave the site of Cannon Hill Park which was honoured by a visit from the Duke of Edinburgh, Queen Victoria's second son, in December of that year. John Holder later added 7 acres 7 perches to its extent. Calthorpe Park was given to the people of Balsall Heath in 1893.

When Salisbury Road was cut local people feared that the pool in Moseley Park, thus separated from the Hall, would be built on so a group of gentlemen formed the Moseley Park and Pool Estate Company and obtained a lease for 40 years. The new private park for Moseley residents was opened by Austen Chamberlain and proved very popular as it included the lake, the remains of the bluebell woods and various other natural attractions for all ages.

Local Government had developed to keep pace with the growing population. Moseley sent one district councillor to the Worcestershire County Council established in 1888. As a result of the 1894 Local Government Act, Kings Norton was controlled by the Kings Norton Rural District Council which employed a clerk, medical officer, hospital officer, surveyor and sanitary inspector with appropriate staffs. On this body Moseley was represented by three Councillors, who also sat on the Board of Guardians of Kings Norton Poor Law Union. It is significant that in 1896 they were described as a farmer, an accountant and a gentleman. Five other men, including the Rev. W. H. Colmore, represented Moseley on Kings Norton Parish Council although female ratepayers, married or single, were allowed by the 1894 Act both to vote and to sit.

Moseley people had feared annexation to Birmingham since the 1870's, believing that the character of the area and of its population were very different from those of the vast industrial city, but in 1911 Kings Norton, including Moseley, and Yardley were among the areas absorbed.

Moseley people had every opportunity for active leisure in the period 1853 to 1914. The many prosperous families enjoyed church activities, private dances such as that held by Mrs. Daniels at Sorrento for seventy in 1894, "at homes" and the annual bonfires at Greenhill School which began in 1881. Several Wake Green Road houses had billiards rooms and "The Moseley Society Journal" commented on the use of one such on a Sunday and on young people walking around in tennis clothes at the hour of evensong. Family occasions were well celebrated and one may read accounts of weddings and even of the twenty-first birthday celebrations of Miss Jessica Eyles in 1912, whose party saw "Kismet" at the Royal Theatre in Birmingham and followed it by supper at the Grand Hotel there.

They must have gone out frequently to enjoy organised functions. Many took place under the auspices of the Moseley and Balsall Heath Institute, founded in 1876 and housed in 1883 in an interesting building which survives today, decorated with heads of Shakespeare and Michelangelo and reliefs of mediaeval scenes symbolising the pursuit of various arts and sciences.

The less fashionable Kings Heath and Moseley Institute was founded in 1878 on a site now occupied by Woolworths Store. Private parties were held there, as well as educational and social functions, for which the Moseley Botanical Gardens, formerly Spring Hill College and now Moseley Grammar School was also popular.

The Rev. W. H. Colmore of St. Mary's was very keen on amateur drama and seems to have founded the Moseley Amateur Drama Society in 1882 *to* pay for church projects. Other groups included the Moseley Shakespearian Society. Some performances were evidently catastrophic as in 1894 when poor Miss Kemp lost hat, sleeve and control of her long hair. Yet plays of all standards were produced by amateurs and presumably watched by their local friends: "Romeo and Juliet" and "Julius Caesar", Pinero's "Magistrate" and Goldsmith's "She stoops to conquer".

Professional concerts were frequently held but amateurs formed the South Birmingham Orchestra Union, which included ladies in the 1890's. Moseley Choral Society, founded in 1886, performed Sterndale Bennett's "May Queen" in 1898 and "Messiah" in 1899. Moseley Musical Club offered "Acis and Galatea" in 1910. These performances were evidently of reasonable standard but the local critic scolded the Mozart Mite Minstrels with "for a short time at a bazaar or school entertainment the company would no doubt win a favourable reception, but to entertain an audience of some 500 people is overtaxing their capabilities to an alarming degree".

Literary Societies were very popular. The Moseley and Balsall Heath Literary Association, in existence by 1877, was copied by Baptist, Methodist and Presbyterian Literary Societies before 1900.

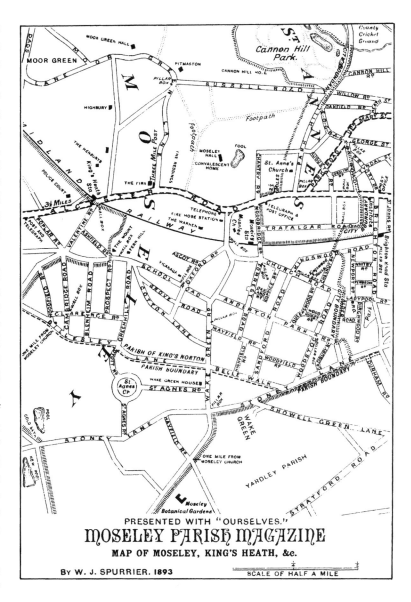

PRESENTED WITH "OURSELVES."
MOSELEY PARISH MAGAZINE
MAP OF MOSELEY, KING'S HEATH, &c.
BY W. J. SPURRIER. 1893
SCALE OF HALF A MILE

The Photographic Society received its impetus from J. Hall-Edwards, L.R.C.P.,F.R.P.S. who wrote and lectured indefatigably on the subject, but it closed due to apathy in 1899.

Politics were organised early. In 1866 eighty men met in the Sherbourne Hotel, Balsall Heath, to discuss the Franchise Bill and petition the House of Commons in support. In March 1874 the Moseley Liberal Association was founded at the Trafalgar Hotel and in April of the same year the Moseley Conservative Association at the Fighting Cocks. In 1907 a Moseley and Kings Heath Parliament is mentioned and the Kings Heath and Moseley Debating Society existed at least from 1909 to 1912.

It is interesting to find that the ladies of Moseley were politically awakened. In May 1909 a large number went to Park House on the Alcester Road to hear Lady Isabel Margesson and Miss Gladice Keevil speaking for the National Women's Social and Political Union and a number enrolled; that year Lady Isabel and Mrs. Bertrand Russell spoke at the home of Dr. Olive Good. In 1913 the local suffragettes put small shot in Salisbury and Amesbury Roads keyholes!

It was a keen sporting area, presumably because such a large proportion of the population had achieved success in business by the time they arrived and so had money and time to spare. As early as 1855 there were cricket clubs, named after Moseley and Balsall Heath, which held a match. In 1858 the Pickwick Club was founded at St. Paul's Road and later removed to Bournbrook. Moseley Cricket Club was formed in 1864 and in 1878 the

Australians paid it their first visit. Moseley Football Club was formed in 1870 and in 1879 defeated the Maoris. Moseley Golf Club opened in 1892 at Billesley Hall Farm and by 1901 there were 44 gentlemen and 30 lady members. Moseley Park Lawn Tennis Club held its first annual tournament at the Reddings in 1886 and Moseley Harriers were pioneers who won the National Cross Country Championship every year from 1881 to 1884. Other organised sports were Bowls and Quoits, Ladies' Hockey in 1909, a Gentlemen's Swimming Club which existed at least from 1908 to 1912, and the Shooting Club mentioned in 1911. In 1896 Moseley Ladies formed a cycling club for fifty members, excluding young girls. Stamina was tested as the programme was likely to include runs as far as Stratford, Clent, Leamington and Bidford-on-Avon.

In 1893 Moseley & Kings Heath Gentlemen's Club opened to combine various activities. Entry cost 2 guineas and there was a further annual subscription of 2 guineas but the member might enjoy billiards, cards, bowls, smoking concerts, the reading room and the restaurant. By 1905 motoring was becoming the rage locally. Evidently Mr. Percy Lea had the first car in Moseley but in that year the Motor Works were opened.

Most of these activities were presumably available only for the prosperous. The poorer Mosleyites could enjoy the pleasure grounds opened in 1861 at the Fighting Cocks and perhaps the Birmingham and Midland Zoological Gardens of Mr. Roberts, the enterprising licensee of the Sherbourne Hotel, who was refused a theatre licence. In 1875 a skating rink opened in Trafalgar Road. The great public parks were also available to all. Then in 1886 the Moseley Working Men's Club was formed at the suggestion of the prosperous and met for eleven years over stables until premises were provided in 1898. In 1891 a Working Girls' Club was established. Presumably all classes joined in the Horticultural Shows held by various organisations from 1860 onwards and there was the South Birmingham Gardeners' Mutual Aid and Improvement Association which was affected by apathy by 1900.

The cinema must have thrilled all alike. In 1912 the first opened in Kings Heath. Tickets cost 3d or 6d and there were two programmes weekly of films such as "The Prison on the Cliff" and "Vengeance of the Mafia". Two more cinemas opened in 1914, one in Balsall Heath and a second in Kings Heath.

Early in this period most social problems were connected with Balsall Heath. By 1862 the leading residents of that area were sufficiently worried about conditions to obtain the establishment of the Balsall Heath Sanitary Board as allowed by the 1848 Public Health Act. This was to consist of nine members elected for 3 year terms, who met monthly. They took their work very seriously until Balsall Heath was annexed by Birmingham in 1891.

Sanitation was a major problem. In 1870 there were sewage floods in Ladypool Lane. In 1872 and 1875 there were serious typhoid epidemics for which contaminated milk from local farms, Moseley dumb wells and ash privies and Brighton Road piggeries may all have been responsible. In 1896 a scarlet fever epidemic was linked with Wake Green Road refuse tips so the more salubrious Moseley was not unscathed, although outside the Balsall Heath Sanitary Board's sphere.

The poor suffered grievously in cold winters and epidemics. Moseley and Balsall Heath were in the Kings Norton Poor Law Union with Smethwick, Edgbaston, Harborne, Northfield and Beoley. The workhouse was in Selly Oak and there were children's cottage homes at Shenley Fields. Balsall Heath people must often have felt that the officials at Kings Norton were not interested and so the local Sanitary Board concerned itself with an ever-increasing range of questions. In 1878 it ensured the opening of Mary Street and Clifton Road schools and Tindal Street followed in the same year as Moseley Church School was obviously inadequate when Balsall Heath population numbered 13,500 by 1870 and continued to grow rapidly. The Relieving Officer opened offices in Woodbridge Road which housed also the Public Vaccinator, the Registrar, Overseers of the Poor and the Rate Collector. The local branch of the Charity Organisation Society must have been overwhelmed with casework from 1880 onwards. The Police force was steadily augmented. Yet in 1870 the residents of Balsall Heath asked for a pound to be provided for stray animals, as the one in Kings Norton was inconveniently far away, and as late as 1882 the area was designated as suffering from Foot and Mouth Disease.

Moseley people must have been involved in Balsall Heath problems until 1891 and even afterwards, particularly because her own poor "can be counted on 10 fingers" in 1895. In the same year only thirty-four pupils required places in the National School and a local government report declared that the majority of Moseley children "were not of the class who required elementary schools." In 1909 there was considerable concern over the land allocated for the upkeep of "the Moseley poor" as few recognised that these existed. Possibly there was much hidden poverty, even among former occupants of large houses whose incomes were dwindling.

There must have been many events which local people found noteworthy but of which the records are lost. National occasions were celebrated with enthusiasm after organisation by careful committees. In 1887 occurred Queen Victoria's Golden Jubilee so £170 was raised to provide meals for the aged poor and a tea for 5,000 children. Ten years later £250 was necessary when the children walked in procession to a field at Moor Green for tea and sports while the old ate at home. Enough money was left to pay for a drinking trough and fountain to stand on the Village Green and to help the Moseley Working Men's Club obtain premises of its own. No records of local celebrations for King Edward VII's Coronation are available but those for his son George V in 1911 were one of the last big events before the War of 1914. There were church services for all; the Kings Heath Brass Band played on the Green; the children received commemorative medals before marching to tea and sports once more; the old of Kings Heath were feasted and special celebrations were held for the little patients of Moseley Hall.

A delightful occasion must have been the Garden Party given by the Moseley Park and Pool Company in 1903. There was a swimming exhibition, a Punch and Judy show, a display of conjuring by Herr Blitz, concerts of glees by the Moseley Quartette and of martial music by the City of Birmingham Military Band and finally illuminations, presumably by the lake.

There must have been great excitement when the first aeroplanes were seen in Moseley skies. On 17th, 18th and 19th July, 1913, Mr. Hicks was observed flying at 70 m.p.h. in what "The Moseley Society Journal" described as a Gnome Tandem military type Bleriot". In September the Village's own aviator Edwin Prosser was seen aloft and a year later he tried, unsuccessfully alas, to deliver golf balls by air to Birmingham clubs.

Some local people became notorious. In 1889 Henry Beresford Moore of Trafalgar Road, known as "the Moseley Baronet," was sentenced for fraud-but then the local M.P. George Hastings was sentenced to 5 years in 1892 for misappropriating trust funds. There was an unfortunate lady in Church Road who had to be restrained from throwing objects into a neighbour's garden in 1895. Poor Mrs. Godfrey's case aroused a local furore in the same year when she was accused of picking pockets at a garden party held at Highbury. As the woman seemed to be very respectable strong feelings were aroused and meetings to ensure justice were held even in Wake Green Road mansions. Eventually the offending sergeant was transferred to a less hostile area and his victim's later life is lost in obscurity.

So much happened in the history of Saint Mary's between 1853 and the outbreak of the First World War in 1914 that one has to divide the period by the three incumbencies of the Reverend J. R. Davison, 1852 to 1876, the Reverend and later Canon W. H. Colmore, 1876 to 1907, and the Reverend and later Archdeacon C. E. Hopton 1907 to 1927. The three men were very different in character and therefore in their contributions to church and Moseley life.

The Reverend John Robert Davison M.A. (Oxon) lived first at Woodfield on Stoney Lane and then in the new parsonage in School Lane. His route to St. Mary's lay either along School Lane and Wake Green Road or by the field footpath which was to become Oxford Road. As late as 1931 an old parishioner wrote of his sense of humour and the account of his funeral in September 1876 described the universal local mourning as his coffin was carried by his choirmen, led by the Cross and followed by twenty-four clergy, from the Parsonage to the Church. His daughter Nora became a painter who sold her work to Queen Victoria and Prince Henry of Battenburg. Otherwise it is known that Mr. Davison was adjudged bankrupt in 1866 and able to pay only 3/- in the £.

He became curate in charge of Moseley Chapel in 1852 just before its change of status in 1853 and was therefore first vicar in 1866. He must have done much to guide the rapidly growing congregation in adding to the dignity of St. Mary's. In 1853 the first organ, said to be of notably sweet tone, was installed and John Barford became organist until 1867. In 1857 subscribers paid for the clock on the tower which must have been useful, especially to the poor. In 1866 gas lighting was provided so evening services became possible and the choir, formerly in the South Gallery, moved to the front of the nave following a contemporary trend to formalise services. In 1870 the nave was enlarged, a clerestory was added and a parapet and pinnacles decorated the top of the tower. A gate was built where two cottages had formerly stood. In 1872 the chancel was extended by 21 feet and soon lit by five windows to the memories of Miss Anderton, Miss Charlotte Thrupp the school mistress, A. Lyndon the solicitor, Horatio Southall and the Reverend J. P. Davison himself. Finally in 1875 the ancient bells were replaced by eight cast in Sheffield steel.

In 1857 Edward Dickenson was appointed as beadle. He was expected to dig graves for a fee of 2/- for five feet and 6d for each additional foot, to keep the churchyard in order and to care for paths and steps for £1 a year. His resplendent uniform of blue coat, red collar, brass buttons and brass studded staff was intended to awe the parishioners, especially if young. He also tried to control the senior members of the choir who fell into the amazing habit of slipping out of church by a side door and into the Bull's Head during sermons. Although unable to stop them he would recall them with "Now, gentlemen, it's come to thirdly. . ." but once the Vicar locked them all out until the service ended. The consequent embarrassment was unfortunately not recorded.

Thomas Averhill died in 1867 aged 78. He had been clerk and sexton of the Chapel for forty-five years. He was succeeded by James Bullock, the successful builder. Other appointments were of an organ blower paid £2 p.a. and two pew openers paid £5 p.a. from 1874.

Saint Mary's Church was no longer adequate to serve the whole District Chapelry when houses of all sizes were erected in outlying areas. In 1860 a chapel of ease dedicated to All Saints was provided in Kings Heath. In 1863 this became the Chapelry of All Saints and in 1866 an independent parish. Its boundary with St. Mary's lay along the modern Dad's Lane, Queensbridge Road and Greenhill Road.

In 1875 the Chapelry of St. Anne's was created. Its church, the gift of Miss Rebecca Anderton, had been built on land presented by W. F. Taylor and consecrated in 1874.

The parish church had been the only religious centre in the District Chapelry of Moseley in 1853 but as the population grew it was inevitable that other denominations should found their own churches and institutions. In 1857 Spring Hill College was opened for Congregational theological training and was described as being built in fifteenth century style round three sides of a quadrangle. The Congregational Church sold it in 1882 and it had various uses including that of Botanical Gardens before it became Moseley Grammar School in 1923. In 1861 a Congregational chapel was opened in Moseley Road.

The Reverend William H. Colmore was born in 1848 of the local family after whom Colmore Row, Birmingham is named and he was educated at Rugby School and St. John's College, Oxford. In later years his appearance was said to be very like that of Edward VII. He was presented to the living by his father-in-law, the Vicar of Bromsgrove, and found it worth £300 p.a. The population of the Moseley Parish numbered 1,500.

Canon Colmore, as he became in 1905, was evidently interested and a leader in all aspects of contemporary life in Moseley. He was to be described as "cheerful, light of touch, optimistic, practical". Records such as his own logbook give an impression of a warm, lively ever active man whose religion was expressed not only in the usual services of a priest but by constant efforts to raise the standard of living for the poor and to encourage enjoyment of the arts. Life at St. Mary's must have been full of colour and excitement without an embarrassing amount of soul searching.

Canon Colmore belonged to the Conservative Association and became President of the local branch. In 1894 he was the chairman of a meeting to demand district councillors for Moseley according to the 1894 Local Government Act and in 1898 he was elected for Moseley Ward to the Kings Norton Parish Council. He was on the Kings Norton School Board from 1877 and became its chairman in 1895. He was Honorary Secretary of the Kings Heath and Moseley Institute from its foundation and so instrumental in arranging a wide range of cultural and educational activities there. He was concerned in the Sherborne Road (Balsall Heath) Dispensary, whose subscribers obtained a little medical aid, and he campaigned for a cabmen's shelter to be built in the Village. He was described as "actual and responsible manager" of the Moseley Amateur Dramatic Society in 1882, as this group performed to finance various church projects, and there is a very noticeable emphasis on musical activities such as choral and other concerts.

In the parish magazine, which he started in December 1878 as people claimed ignorance of events and he wished to draw the congregation together, Canon Colmore gave vivid descriptions of events in Church life, many of which he originated.

On Dec. 31st 1878 he held the first recorded Moseley midnight service and wrote of the "solemnity quite indescribable of the closing minutes of the year; and the solemn tolling of the bell as the whole congregation knelt in silent prayer". Harvest Festivals began in 1878. The harvest was disappointing in 1879 so no festival was held but in September 1880 he wrote of very large congregations at all the services. He was delighted by decorations for special occasions. For the 1880 Harvest Festival the Screen was ornamented with wheat and oats, maize and trailing grasses . . . "and the pulpit and lectern harmoniously decorated with hops, bunches of grapes and dahlias of a rich deep red". At Christmas 1882 the altar vases were filled with white camellias, each bouquet offset by a single red flower; the pulpit was covered with white and red helichrysum "worked in symbolic patterns" and on the verge were yellow and white chrysanthemums.

In January 1879 the first Parish Tea was held and the event became so popular that eventually he had to issue tickets to those entitled to attend. Entertainments soon formed an evidently successful pattern of songs, short plays and operettas with forgotten titles such as "Off Duty", "On the Sly", "Medicine Jack" and "Two Lunatics"; the dancing of little Miss Thomas "which electrified the company", and the Moseley Hand Bell Ringers from 1883 onwards. There were occasional innovations such as the conjuror, Herr Blitz, in 1890 but the reports always give an impression of wholesome if simple gaiety.

Rather exclusive Annual Conversaziones were held at the Kings Heath and Moseley Institute from 1902 until 1910 and the minute book is full of evocative detail. The ladies chose special colour schemes for decorations and programmes: pale blue and pink in 1906, blue and yellow in 1907, green and white in 1908. Tickets at 2/6 included suppers of oyster patties, champagne jelly and "French and German pastries". In addition, champagne cost 10/- for a large bottle but brandy or whiskey was 6d a glass. They waltzed to "The Blue Danube" and "The Eton Boating Song" and always included the Lancers. Whist prizes were bought with care: two silver butter knives for 10/6, a silk umbrella for 14/- or glove and handkerchief cases.

Choir outings appear to have begun in 1879 and were often organised by Mr. Kynnersley of Moor Green. Boys and men had separate expeditions to Oxford, Malvern, Chepstow, Matlock and even Belvoir Castle. At Worcester in 1884 Mr. H. Hooper lost his hat in the river, and at Rhyl in the same year everyone missed the train home because one boy had returned to the Punch & Judy Show. Some boys bathed in the river eight times in one day at Shrewsbury in 1889, and the men sang at every station on their journey home from Tewkesbury in 1892. The choir often took part in choral festivals. Stainer's "Crucifixion" was performed annually at Easter for many years. It was a work meant to raise contemporary standards.

The National Schools children were important in parish life. Concerts were held to pay for library books; Inspectors' reports were printed in the Magazine for all to read; halfpenny dinners were provided by local ladies during cold winters such as 1889 and 1890-91 when the worst frost since 1814 gripped the country from December 1st to January 21st. Annual treats were organised in the grounds of various large houses and though a service might start the proceedings balloons and Kings Heath Band were regular features.

Useful organisations occupied the local women, though social classes were segregated according to contemporary custom. Ladies joined the Needlework Guild (1894) to make at least two garments a year for the poor and they were invited to Tuesday afternoon Bible Classes at the Vicarage. They organised sales of work, such as the one in 1888 when all the stalls were named after the holders' favourite flowers and the goods included kittens, babies' shoes, anti-macassars, dog biscuits and strawberries. They gave the Parish Teas and a few helped to run the eductional Girls' Friendly Society (1883) the Mother's Union (1895) and the Band of Hope (1901). In 1904 the parish adopted the slum parish of Saint Edward's, New John Street West and undertook to run many activities there from clubs to outings.

Children stayed in their own social circles too. In 1896 those who attended Sunday afternoon services which were specifically intended for "children of the better classes" collected pennies to buy extra furnishings for the young patients of Moseley Hall Hospital.

In the surviving parish magazines there is not a great emphasis on spiritual development. Canon Colmore worried about the small number of communicants when he first came to Moseley and in 1880 asked the congregation to be punctual rather than arriving in the middle of the General Confession or Absolution.

The congregation was evidently wealthy, though inevitably much affected by depressions in trade and industry, and willing to make the church beautiful and fitting not only for worship but for their own concept of the community's dignified and prosperous status. In 1884 the North Aisle was built in Perpendicular Style with an open timber roof. The cost was £1,700 and half the seats were to be free. In 1890 the vestry was built for £41 1 and by 1898 the chancel and south transept had been rebuilt. The architect during this period was J. A. Chatwin, F.R.I.B.A.

In 1885 the children of the parish gave a font and ewer and in 1898 a group of ladies presented the pulpit. A new organ had been installed in 1887. Individuals added a brass pulpit desk, brass altar rails and a gas bracket.

Families commemorated their dead with the Lingard window (1890) the Avins window depicting Moses in the bulrushes (1892) and the SneydKynnersley window showing women washing Christ's feet (1893), all in the North aisle. In 1897 a new chancel window with seven lights was built which incorporated the four memorial windows of 1872, and in 1904 the central section of the stone reredos was erected in memory of J. H. Bell, the organist from 1871 until 1903.

By 1876 Kings Norton Sanitary Authority was worried by the overcrowding of St. Mary's cemetery and petitions to the Home Secretary asking for it to be closed were circulated in the Village. Consequently in 1878 the Bishop of Worcester was able to open an extension of 4,494 square yards which had been the site of the seven cottages and gardens often associated with the Bull's Head.

St. Agnes Church was founded as there was a rapidly increasing population in "Moseley in Yardley" beyond Billesley Lane. The first building was a temporary wooden structure at the corner of Oxford and School Roads and Canon Colmore was anxious to make it as attractive as possible. In 1884 it was possible for the Bishop to consecrate the permanent St. Agnes Church designed by Mr. W. Davis.

Not everyone in Moseley attended Church of England Services. In 1888 Moseley Baptist Chapel was built in Oxford Road very near St. Mary's and in 1897 the foundation stone was laid of the hall of the Presbyterian Congregation at the top of the new Chantry Road. It would be interesting to know if the local clergy had much contact with each other. The obituary in the parish magazine of 1907 describes Canon Colmore as "a man of moderation who had the respect of churchmen of all schools, and of Nonconformists as well".

In June 1907 the Vicar had died after a short illness. An eye witness can still vividly evoke the day of his funeral when heavy rain fell on crowds of Church dignitaries and grieving villagers, massed flowers and streets where all business had ceased.

The next incumbent was the Reverend Charles E. Hopton and all available sources indicate that there was a sudden change in the life of Saint Mary's and probably of Moseley. He was an austere, rather rigid and very conscientious man who longed for all to accept the same devout way of life which he had adopted himself. He must have given an awesome impression although one former teacher at the Church School still speaks of his warm heart and his ultimate fear that he had failed in the work God intended him to do in the parish.

He prepared the children of the wealthy for confirmation while his curates dealt with their servants but he did organise house-to-house visits in 1911 and 1913 and made all pews on the right hand side of the Church free to end the unseemly scramble for vacant seats which followed the entry of the clergy in Canon Colmore's day when only a few pews at the back of the North Aisle and under the gallery were free. He frequently urged parishioners to help the poor more, such as "Birmingham Street Children", and was anxious to develop the work in the two Birmingham parishes adopted by St. Mary's and St. Agnes congregations in 1904: St. Edward's, New John Street West, and St. Andrew's, Bordesley. There Moseley people ran Sunday Schools, Creches, girls' and mothers' clubs, billiards and gymnastics for men, Christmas and summer outings and provided clothing and notes for Hospital treatment.

Archdeacon Hopton, as he became in 1916, was High Church in outlook though his interest was in the spiritual aspect, and he did not use incense or elaborate vestments. Throughout his vicarate in Moseley he stressed the need for self-discipline and self-denial, especially in Lent when he advised special programmes of worship, prayer, fasting, alms giving, absence from purely social gatherings, and reading which excluded novels. In 1911 he introduced confession and asked parishioners to list all their sins from childhood. Eventually about twenty made regular confessions to him and a few continued after he retired to Edgbaston. He wanted people to make regular use of the daily services of Communion, Matins and Evensong and asked Sunday communicants to attend Saturday evening services of preparation. In 1909 he arranged a parish mission which was well attended but did not lead to an improvement in numbers of communicants or church attendances.

Established events such as the Conversaziones, the Parish Tea and various treats continued but were more disciplined and probably less spontaneously joyful than before 1907. Those attending the second event had to pay 6d. a ticket and could no longer persuade the clergy to allow their children admission. Nor could they take home food, though various ladies were now responsible for specific tables and competed in generosity. Sunday School children were not eligible for outings unless they had been class members for at least three months and had a 75% attendance record, and they received commendations, then medals, rather than the book prizes which meant so much to clever but poor children far from a public library. Lecture programmes were provided on missionary topics, such as the Chinese and the Eskimos, but attendances were small even when topics such as Aeroplanes and Stars and lantern shows of sacred paintings were offered.

Various new organisations were developed. The Parish Board of Missions was appointed in 1909. The United Parish Organisation for men was founded in 1907 but replaced by the Church of England Men's Society which discussed current controversies such as the 1912 Bill to ensure that only undenominational religious education was given in Schools where there was no alternative free educational provision, or the proposals to make divorce easier. At the latter meeting in 1913 Moseley men evidently agreed that "divorce was an abominable thing and should not be permitted in any shape, and that women should be given no further rights than they at present held". There was also a Young Men's Bible Class and in 1914 the Church Lads' Brigade was formed with the Archdeacon's comment that "the best way to bring up lads between 14 and 19 is to teach rigid discipline". Children might join the King's Messengers, an organisation intended to interest them in the mission field, and the segregated Sunday schools continued in such a way that surviving teachers of one group cannot remember hearing anything about the other, though teachers' successes in national Scripture examinations were much approved.

Though parish dramatic efforts evidently declined, music was still important in parish life. There were special performances of selections from the "Messiah", J. F. Bridge's "Cradle of Christ" and inevitably Stainer's "Crucifixion". There was a "Select Choir" which performed at a Worcester festival and also a Madrigal Society. In 1909 Archdeacon Hopton had written "Our generation, more than most, is beset with difficulties intellectual, moral and practical." In 1914 he wrote that he believed that the decline in church attendance was due to the number of amusements available: cars, trains, picture houses and music halls.

Archdeacon Hopton was very anxious to complete the church and became involved in plans shortly after arriving but he gave priority to the provision of the "church rooms" which were ready by March 1908. He believed that the temporary building's lack of beauty was unimportant considering its utility and it certainly was much used until 1969.

In 1909, at a cost of over £7,000, St. Mary's was almost rebuilt and Rickman's renovations of cast iron, low ceiling, mock oak beams and plastered walls disappeared. The present nave and clerestory and the south aisle were erected. The results were curiously described as making the church "sanitary". Canon Colmore was commemorated by a South Aisle window and side panels added to the reredos. Similar panels honoured the organist Mr. Bell. In 1913 the South Aisle window depicting the Baptism of Christ was dedicated to the memory of Thomas Grimley and battlements were added to the tower. The question of installing electric light at a cost of £150 divided the parochial council equally so Archdeacon Hopton cast his vote against, though it is evident that he would have liked the innovation.

The congregation faced great expense in connection with the Church School. In 1910 the Board of Education insisted that the boys' school must be enlarged, new infant premises must be provided and the offices must be moved at a cost of £1,700. Walter F. Hook's nephew preached at a special appeal service but a grand Bazaar was necessary. Mr Taylor sold the freehold of the site to the Church for £150, a great bargain as the lease would have lapsed in 1927.

In 1910 St. Agnes Church was recognised as serving a Conventional Ecclesiastical District and in 1914 it became an independent parish. St. Mary's parishioners had worked very hard to found the prosperous community. Their attention turned to the provision of the church for the Moor Green area as the Russells had given a site, but this was never to be used.

In 1909 the Swedenborgian New Church was built at the Alcester Road end of Reddings Road. The congregation had been formed in 1879.

CHAPTER VII.

THE FIRST WORLD WAR 1914 - 1918

Moseley's experience in the First World War must have been common with those of many similar communities in Britain, but the dry details of official accounts became poignant when considered in the context of local families and organisations. Presumably contemporary opinion was reflected in the articles written by Archdeacon Hopton for the parish magazine and by the editor of the Moseley & Kings Heath Society Journal. At first there was a sense of almost divine mission and exaltation.

The Parish magazine printed the Archbishop of Canterbury's declaration of June 1915: "I am certain that in opposing with every power at our command the forces which seem to have set themselves to defy the sacred principles of honour and right which He taught us for the bettering of the world, we are beyond all question acting as we ought". The Vicar himself wrote in January 1915 that there would be "no nobler page of England's life than that which will describe all that her sailors and soldiers have done for her during the last five months". As the weary struggle wore on it was realised that victory would be hard to win. There was anxiety in every home and no attempt to pretend that life was not gloomy and difficult. The comfortable, well organised, self-confident life of many Moseley families was disrupted but the community was united socially as never before. At first publications record the activities of the middle class but gradually awareness of the courage and achievements of the ranks gives them their place in the obituaries and reports of awards and of life at the Front. Almost everyone seems to have been involved in the war effort in some capacity.

Most Moseley men were quick to "join the colours". All the eligible members of Ashfield Cricket Club enlisted together and the sons of many well-known local families went to the Public Schools or City Battalions before the end of 1914. The Moseley Volunteer Training Corps was founded and the Moseley Rifle Corps "to strengthen Kitchener's Army and contribute to home defence". There were scathing comments on those still seen in civilian clothing.

Prominent people lent their houses for hostel and hospital accommodation. Sir John Holder's Moor Green House became first a hostel for Belgian refugees' families and then a hospital for officers staffed by Moseley girls organised by Mrs. Lea. Stanley House, at the corner of Wake Green and Mayfield Road, was a Belgian hostel but closed in December 1915. The Chamberlain homes became hospitals. Highbury was run by V.A.D's for general, then neurological and finally orthopaedic cases and the famous orchid houses became wards, while Moor Green Hall was run by tbe Red Cross.

Uffculme was a hostel then a hospital run by the Society of Friends. The Dingle became a nursing home. In addition, the future Moseley Grammar School was a military depot. The Village must have become familiar to men from all over Britain.

Adults who stayed at home were very active. They organised the hospitals described above. They worked for the Moseley Auxiliary Branch of the Birmingham Citizens' Committee, raising funds by bazaars and newspaper sales, collecting books and records for the Fleet and razor blades for the Lord Mayor's Appeal, sewing for the forces and training to nurse if required. The Belgian Refugee Home Committee was chaired by Sir John Holder and the minutes indicate how much care was expended to make the foreigners comfortable. They included a priest, a doctor, two veterinary surgeons, a brewer, a teacher and a countess. They were provided with varied goods on Pound Day but expected to earn a living, and soon able men among them were urged to join the armed forces. The Girls' Friendly Society, whose members had very low wages, raised £1.3. o. for Princess Mary's Christmas Present Fund in late 1914, and sent fifteen knitted scarves, ten pairs of socks and seven pairs of mittens to a Transportation Hospital in France. Local schoolchildren formed Concert parties to entertain patients in the temporary hospitals and also the Belgian refugees. The National Service Poultry Club tried to support the war effort by producing extra food.

Propaganda and rumour were rife even among such busy people. There were stories of enemy brutality and bad manners which included statements such as "It is no uncommon sight in Antwerp to see Germans bayonetting defenceless dogs", and even in 1919 there was an attempt to discredit German nation toys. It was suggested in a magazine that Dr. Crippen was of that nation. The patriotism of people with foreign names was doubted and a local tradesman had to display his birth certificate to prove that he had been born in Ladywood, although his father came from Brussels. By late 1918 the danger - had changed character: there were rumours of a Bolshevik gang lurking in Strensham Hill.

There was an attempt to maintain some social activities at first. The Moseley Ladies' Hockey club fixtures were held and the Moseley Musical Club Concert season and programmes of lectures, whist drives and even a Dickens evening and a Conversazione kept the Institutes open, but Moseley Hall Gymkhana was not held. Even journeys into Birmingham must have been more difficult than in peace-time for though the trams continued the cabhorses of Moseley Mews had been commandeered by the Army in September 1914 and men servants eligible for service had enlisted with their masters' sons. Magazine advertisements extolled the value of gas appliances in keeping scarce servants happy. Most families were soon wearing mourning black and entertaining was limited. Building had ceased except for the new Post Office on the Alcester Road, which was opened in 1915.

At St. Mary's special services were introduced as soon as war broke out. The bells were rung daily at noon when special intercessions were said and in September 1915 there was a week of prayer and self-discipline. Humility was demanded as "we are realising that this issue (victory) will not be attained without far greater sacrifices ... and perhaps even for a time more serious setbacks than was at first believed possible." The League of Honour was formed whose members promised "by the help of God to do all that is in my power to uphold the honour of our Empire and its defenders in time of war by Prayer, Purity and Temperance". Lists of those on active service, in prisoner-of-war camps and believed dead were printed in every issue of the Church magazine with moving obituaries for former members of the choir. Lantern lecture programmes provided by "The Daily Mail" showed "How the British Soldier fights", "How British pluck won through in France", "Fire and Sword in Belgium" and "The Kaiser's Blow at Britain: the Fight for the Straits of Dover". Eventually the popular curate J. L. Cappell joined up as a chaplain and died of pneumonial meningitis in 1918.

Most of the established Church activities continued under difficulties. Music for the month is not listed after May 1916 so probably the choir was by then seriously depleted, whereas in summer 1915 the men had enjoyed their annual outing. Sunday School classes were still important in parish life and the children's treats were held although in 1917 and 1918 the Parish Teas for adults were made impossible by food restrictions. C.E.M.S., C.L.B., Scouts and missionary study circles met as usual. In July 1915 a Missionary Pageant was performed in the Vicarage garden to illustrate the history of the Church in England. Scenes depicting Druid sacrifices, Joseph of Arimathea bringing the Holy Grail to Glastonbury and the signing of Magna Carta were accompanied by selections from a string orchestra. Perhaps any soldiers present on leave were able to forget the war for an hour.

Work in the Church did not halt completely. The Walker Screen was erected between the Lady Chapel and the South aisle and in 1916 a window was erected in the latter to the memory of young Douglas Greenaway of the Worcester Regiment, killed at Gallipoli. At the West End a window was added in memory of Mrs. Tippetts but it was to be almost destroyed in World War II. As early as January 1918 it was decided that the parish War memorial should be a new Church Hall and the Calvary which now stands in the churchyard. The latter was commissioned from the Bromsgrove Guild, in Portland stone. When the Armistice was announced in November 1918 the men of Moor Green House hospital danced on the lawns for joy and the streets were illuminated, but the War had changed much in Moseley for ever.

CHAPTER VIII.

MOSELEY 1920 - 1945
DEPRESSION AND WAR

Surviving Servicemen returned to a Moseley which was no longer an independent village but gradually becoming a suburb of Birmingham. Her links with the City had been strengthened during the War when everyone was made aware of events far beyond the Parish boundary and the population's will to help the war effort had been organised on a national scale. As men of importance died their families deserted the largest houses for homes elsewhere, probably further out into the countryside of Warwickshire. Many well known names disappeared from local life.

Moseley Hall continued to be used as the Children's Convalescent Hospital. Highbury's master Joseph Chamberlain had died in 1914 so it continued as a convalescent home until 1932 when it was given to the City to become an old people's home. The great statesman's study has been preserved as he left it.

Richard Cadbury's Uffculme had been presented to Birmingham in 1916. It became an annexe of All Saints Hospital in 1931 and an early treatment centre for neurosis in 1956. Sorrento became a maternity hospital.

In 1923 Sir John Holder died and his mansion was demolished in 1927 to make way for offices called Pitmaston. Moor Green Hall had already been bought by the Britannic Assurance Company in 1920 and was replaced by a large modern office block before long. The Dingle became a Nursing Home and the charming old red brick house at the junction of Wake Green and Oxford Roads was destroyed to make way for the Meteor Garage.

More modest buildings disappeared too. The ivy-covered cottages shown in a 1912 photograph of Billesley Lane were demolished in 1924 when modern houses replaced the trees and hedges which may have dated from the late eighteenth century enclosure. A brick farmhouse on Wake Green was demolished in 1932 but another still stood in Holder's Lane and there were old cottages at Moor Green in 1933.

The leaders of the old Moseley society were disappearing during the 1920's. The death of Sir John Holder was followed by those of Mr. E. M. Sneyd-Kynnersley, a retired Inspector of Schools for Chester and son of the Stipendiary Magistrate who had been a benevolent influence; Major Francis Hall-Edwards, the Photography and Radiography pioneer; Dr. Gosling of Fivelands who had driven round his medical practice for 45 years in a horse and carriage; Dr. Underhill at the age of 83. Well-known ladies died too. Mrs. Blackham of Forest Road achieved her century after three marriages and with the proud memory of having seen the great Duke of Wellington himself. Mrs. Tipper died at 92 in Moseley although her husband had been well known as the proprietor of a veterinary goods firm in Balsall Heath, founded in 1863, and as a councillor there.

Moseley people still became well known. Sir Barry Jackson, who founded the Birmingham Repertory Theatre in 1913 and later the Malvern Festival, lived at "The Grange" on Wake Green Road when young. Dame Hilda Lloyd, born of the family who owned Shufflebotham's Grocery and Wine stores, was the first woman to preside over any royal college. Older residents could probably suggest many other names such as that of Dr. F. W. Lanchester mentioned in 1929 as "the celebrated Moseley motor engineer."

The depression affected financially many of those who lived in places such as Wake Green Road and they found difficulty in obtaining enough servants to run their spacious homes. Some of the big houses disappeared and others were converted to non-residential purposes. One lady describes the years between the Wars as a dull period when nothing significant happened. Not only had many of the young men been killed but everyone's way of life had changed.

Moseley was still a desirable area to which professional people from other parts of Britain came in search of homes. A high proportion of the residents employed maids and gardeners and a row of nurses sat by the pavilion in the Private Park, watching their charges play on the swings. There must be many snapshots of children of the 1930's with bobbed hair and smocked dresses or shorts and shirts, playing on "the toast rack" and in the bluebell wood or talking to the Park-keeper, who had a magnificent waxed imperial moustache.

It is not difficult to visualise the Village of this period. The 1924 "Moseley and Kings Heath Directory" mentions W. H. Smith the Stationer, the Midland Bank, Wimbush's bakery, George Mason's grocery, Houghton the hosier, Boots' and Lowther's the Chemists, and Garner's Motor Repairs. Other businesses are remembered by many because they have disappeared since the Second World War or their owners lived on in Moseley until recently. There were Miss Young the tiny Chiropodist, the Misses Ayliffe who had come from Gloucestershire to run a baby linen shop, Mr. Marshall the Chemist who displayed the traditional elegant bottles filled with mysterious red and green liquids, Mrs. Leary the greengrocer and fish dealer who filled the author with awe in the late 1940's because she received her customers with almost regal dignity and prided herself on knowing each family's tastes.

Cecil Knight's furniture Showroom stretched out into mysterious gloom and the wet, white slabs of Mr Griffiths, the poulterer, were lit by a flaring gas jet. Shufflebotham's Store was particularly intriguing at Christmas when magnificent crackers were on show. Trams clanked and groaned their way from Town and Balsall Heath but the milkman's carts were drawn by friendly horses.

Moseley must have provided a secure home for many children. Some attended the National School, still in the building of 1828, whose headmaster from 1919 until 1940 was Mr. A. F. Harvey. His salary in 1922 was £10 a week but then he had earned only £8 a year as a pupil teacher in the late nineteenth century. Others were educated at the many private schools which maintained the Moseley tradition. In 1936 there were Woodroughs and New College for boys and Moseley Modern School, Moseley College and St. Hilda's for girls, as well as various "prep" schools. Wintersloe had closed in 1931 and Greenhill School in 1918, five years short of its centenary. Children also travelled to Edgbaston schools in special buses.

Adults might still find their amusements in the Village. Moseley Rugby Football Club, Golf Club and Cricket Club revived after the War. There were several tennis clubs, the Salisbury Bowling Club and the Moseley Quoits and Bowling Club. The Moseley Musical Club also survived and the traditional programmes were carried out at the Moseley and Balsall Heath Institute and the Kings Heath and Moseley Institute, However, most residents must have gone into the City Centre for films, drama, concerts and shopping if the advertisements in "The Birmingham and Moseley Society Journal" are considered as reflecting contemporary interests. That publication mentioned very few local events by the 1930's and was last issued in 1933. Moseley was merging naturally into Birmingham in spite of earlier residents' opposition to the 1911 Greater Birmingham Act.

By 1935 prosperity was returning to the Midlands and the Vicar noted in the St. Mary's magazine that faces were happier, but hope was short-lived. In 1938 came the Munich Crisis and in 1939 the Second World War.

Evacuation of local children began immediately. Many were lined up, labels attached to their clothes, on Moseley Station platform. Older people, especially women, left too afraid that the enemy would bomb industrial centres such as Birmingham immediately. Most of the remaining large houses in the Wake Green Road area were closed and later in the war several were sold and their contents were auctioned. Blackout was organised and wardens were appointed to keep watch for lights and fires. Public air-raid shelters were opened at Moseley Hall Hospital, Uffculme and the junction of Wake Green and Yardley Wood Roads. Many residents had small shelters built in their gardens or reinforced their cellars. An air-raid siren was installed.

Eventually the "Moseley Fire Party" built a fire engine at the Park Garage and it was dedicated by the Vicar. Many of the older men were members of the Home Guard and others were organised to deal with emergencies which brought together neighbours who had rarely spoken before the War. The bombing began in 1940 and hostels for the homeless were organised at 29, Chantry Road, and 8, Amesbury Road. Then in 1944, when conventional air raids seemed to be a thing of the past, evacuees from the "buzz bombs" showering on London and the South East came flooding into the area. A party was held for these children in 1945 at which they were given toys and sweets from the U.S.A. and 6d. Saving Stamps. Peace in Europe was celebrated by a Victory party for the children in the summer and a great bonfire in Moseley Park late in the year, but many Moseley people must have taken their children into Birmingham to see the crowds dancing and singing in New Street, even if only from the safety of the IA bus. The local churches were packed for the services of thanksgiving.

Life at St. Mary's Parish Church changed in many ways as the "old" Moseley families left and a more democratic and egalitarian society developed in the area. Archdeacon Hopton's last years here were probably sad as he worried about changing standards and rising costs of maintaining the buildings in his care. His magazine editorials also indicate the community's increased awareness of problems beyond the parish boundary as he wrote about the Peace Conference at Versailles, troubles in Ireland, unemployment and the General Strike of 1926. There was a Parish Working Party to aid refugees in Central Europe although help was still given to the adopted parish of St. Edward's, New John Street West. Others were involved in St. Mary's Guild, the Church Lads' Brigade, the Girls' Friendly Society, the Church of England Men's Society, the Mothers' Union, Sunday School teaching etc. Pageants, Summer Markets and Socials were held but it is obvious from magazine reports that they were shadows of pre-war activities.

The 1922 diamond wedding celebrations of the Verger, Mr. Charles Cross, must have revived many memories. He had worked at the Church since 1872, first as pew opener and bell ringer and then Verger from 1897 until 1931. He must have been a well known figure in Moseley in old age, when he wore a skull cap and smoked a clay pipe. Various photographs indicate strong character: he is said to have kept the Tower clock going by striking it with a hammer. He was to die in 1931 in his 94th year: the oldest Verger in England. His daughter Charlotte Cross succeeded him as Verger. She gave his treasured handbells to St. Mary's.

Various plans made before or during the War had to be postponed because of the general scarcity of money in the 1920's. It was not possible to rebuild the Church Rooms in Oxford Road as part of Moseley's war memorial because the cost of £4,000 was too great for the congregation. In 1926 all hope of building a new daughter church in the Russell Road area was abandoned and the site reverted to the Russell Estate Trustees. Panelling of the Sanctuary walls began as a memorial to Mr. M. P. Lea and carved altar rails and standard candlesticks were given to commemorate his wife.

In 1927 Archdeacon Hopton was succeeded by Canon A. N. Bax, M.A. His magazine articles suggest a kindly, artistic man because he wrote sensitive obituaries and sometimes included his own poems. He seemed particularly interested in youth work as the St. Mary's Junior Brotherhood was formed; the Scout Troop was encouraged and Companies of Brownies and Guides developed. In the inauspicious year of 1939 the interdenominational Moseley Youth Movement was founded under the leadership of Mr. R. E. Green and became an important factor in social life for many young Moseley people, in spite of the Second World War and the fact that few of those born or brought up in Moseley now spent their adult lives in the locality. Adult activities continued on the usual lines except that a Guild of Tapisters was formed to work hassocks and Bridge evenings were occasionally held to raise money for purposes such as the renovation of the Church Rooms. In 1935 tickets for these occasions cost 3/6d and evening dress was optional.

As in 1914, St. Mary's was a centre of activity in the Second World War. Ignorant optimism was no longer possible for intelligent people so Canon Bax wrote "If we win, as God grant we may" then made practical arrangements for Church life to continue as normally as possible-if possible. Congregations were warned that if an air raid began during service they should stay seated, singing hymns, or lie flat on the floor. They should always carry their gas masks. Invitations to a social in 1940 read "Evening Dress optional. Please bring your gasmasks and arrive early".

Male members of the congregation who had not been called up for active service established an advisory service for women left alone to cope with business and family problems. Adolescents over seventeen years of age formed the Messenger Service to carry blood from the Queen Elizabeth Hospital, by bicycle, to First Aid centres after air raids. A branch of the Women's Voluntary Service organised various comforts for the sorely tried population. Servicemen could write to another group whose task was to search for bombed-out relatives of those unable to obtain compassionate leave. By 1944 most of the congregation's energies were absorbed by the war effort and many club and social activities ceased. Life was difficult and often disorganised. Choirboys had to be lured to practice by the promise of tea.

When bombing of Birmingham began in 1940 Canon Bax himself kept watch in the Church. In October an incendiary bomb set fire to a pew, which remains today as a memorial, damaged a pillar and also the roof of the nave. On December 3rd the explosion of a landmine on the far side of the railway line shattered much stained glass in the East window and the North and South windows of the Sanctuary, the North aisle and the Lady

Chapel. The reredos was shaken away from the East wall and eventually proved to be too damaged to restore.

Canon Bax must have found this very distressing as he had tried so hard to beautify the Church building, aided by parishioners who gave memorials in the practical form of Church furnishings. The Lady Chapel had been provided with a War Memorial window, now destroyed, a carved screen and eighteenth century panelling from Saint Bartholomew's Church, Birmingham. Oak doors had been fitted to the Sacristy and Choir Vestry. The stone facing of the North Aisle had been completed as George V lay dying, a circumstance recorded by an inscription by the pulpit. The Misses Anderton had given a Screen to stand between the Chancel and North Aisle and the Prior screen at the east end of the North aisle commemorated the Cornish origin of the man remembered with carvings of anemones, seaweed, sea snails, prawns and pilchards.

Fine churchyard gates designed and made by the Bromsgrove Guild were a memorial to Councillor Frederick Tippetts and the Lych Gate was given in 1933 by the pupils of Mr. Fisher, headmaster of Wintersloe School.

There were many other improvements and Mr. Robert Stevens had bought the cottages between the Church and the Bull's Head to preserve the last of old Moseley's village buildings. Canon Bax must have been relieved when the bombing ceased and much of his work remained. He resigned the living in 1943 and died in 1960.

Miss Charlotte Cross retired as Verger in 1953. She was the granddaughter of William Dickenson, beadle of the mid-nineteenth century, so the last of five generations of her family to serve the parish.

CHAPTER IX.

MOSELEY 1945 - 1970

The next incumbent was Canon C.T. Cribb, a graduate of Durham University, who had worked in Leamington, Oldbury and Smethwick but also in Java. His years in Moseley were in the difficult aftermath of war when the building had to be repaired in spite of general shortages and universal weariness and the congregation had to be inspired to face the disappointments of an uneasy peace. Various stalwarts disappeared over the years. In 1955 Mr. Frank Ford the organist retired. In 1957 died Mr. Robert Stevens, who had been Vicar's Warden for seventeen years until in 1955 he was made Deputy Vicar's Warden for life and who had devoted his retirement to making the churchyard a place where Moseley people found beauty. The Vicar was depressed by a 1951 survey which showed that many people were antagonistic to Church and clergy and he wrote that in "these selfish days, offers of regular service to the Church are rare."

In fact church life continued if in an unspectacular way. Various organisations met regularly: the Mothers Union, the Parochial Board of Missions, the Zenana Missionary Society, the British and Foreign Bible Society, Study Circle and various youth groups. The Youth Movement enjoyed serious programmes such as forums and films on contemporary problems and religious studies. The Mothers Union became the Women's Fellowship to welcome all women and its members also tried to prepare for the new world by enquiring into the work of groups such as the women police. The Bishop's campaigns on behalf of new housing estates, "Circles without Centres" and "The Second Mile Appeal" were well supported but a few members found time in 1956 to help to initiate an interdenominational club to welcome West Indians which met in Balsall Heath and eventually became known as the Happy-Link Club.

Probably the most important development of all was the growth of the local ecumenical movement. In 1941 joint services with Moseley Presbyterians and Baptists on Good Friday and Remembrance Sunday had proved that attitudes had changed radically since the days at the end of the nineteenth century when St. Mary's people seem to have resented the new nonconformist congregations developing in Moseley. This movement has continued to grow until nowadays members of all local churches of any and every denomination gather on Palm Sunday to raise a wooden cross on the remains of the Village Green.

In 1962 the Reverend F. C. Carpenter, M.A., former chaplain of Sherborne School, succeeded Canon Cribb as Vicar of Moseley. He was very anxious to make the congregation think outwardly rather than considering religious observances a soothing routine. He discussed belief, true Church unity, particular services, prayer and many contemporary problems, both religious and of the world at large. He joined in the movement for greater understanding among the denominations, attending the Requiem Mass for Pope John in 1963 with other local Anglican, Baptist and Methodist Clergy, giving much consideration to Anglican-Methodist Reunion and initiating the Procession of Witness on Good Friday, 1968. He believed in a social ministry so developed the growing awareness of the congregation and quoted the Bishop of Chelmsford's statement that the "test of Christian discipleship is neither orthodoxy nor zeal but a limitless caring for people." He believed that laity as well as clergy should be responsible for parochial visiting. A club for the "over-60's" was founded in 1965 and the Shell Club for children from less fortunate areas in 1966. The congregation was awakened to the problems of drug addiction and prostitution which were increasingly prominent in the area.' Yet the arts were not forgotten. Drama became a feature of St. Mary's life once more and it was decided in 1966 to rebuild the venerable organ entirely, a task completed in 1970.

Since the institution of the Reverend Lorys M. Davies in 1968 the social ministry has continued to gain momentum and must surely be of real significance in Moseley. Parochial visiting and co-operation with the various statutory and voluntary agencies are developing continuously. When a new school replaced the little building of W. F. Hook in 1969 it was decided to turn the latter into a community centre with a full time youth leader in the hope that everyone living in Moseley, of any race, colour or creed, would feel welcome there. Devotional expression is still developing too as new ideas are tested and adopted or discarded by democratic discussions which might have horrified incumbents of past centuries. There is a use for every talent: artistic, academic and practical. It is too early to write the history of the 1970's but there is confidence that some future historian will find it deeply interesting.

St. Mary's Church was restored in time for the 550th anniversary of the papal mandate permitting the erection of the original chapel of ease, an occasion which Queen Elizabeth II marked by the gift of a wooden carving of the crowned Virgin by Kramer of Mainz which how hangs in the Chancel. The year before a new East Window had been installed in which the artist Donald Taunton used the Sermon on the Mount to express a love of the English countryside which would have been appreciated by the Grevis and Rotton families and the long dead congregations of rural Moseley. Rabbits, sheep and a sheepdog, kingfishers, ring doves, partridge, pheasant, lapwings and moorhens stand among bluebells, daises, cornflower, speedwell, iris and flowering rushes. But Moseley people now roamed the world so among their flowers were figures in the costumes of Africa, America, China, India, New Zealand, Switzerland, France and Spain attended by the animals familiar to them and by sight at least to us. Other windows were replaced gradually. A silver processional cross, silver candlesticks, a silver alms dish and two handsome staves for the Vicar's Warden and People's Warden were the best known of many gifts. In 1969 the west end of the North Aisle was turned into a comfortable lounge so that meetings and discussions of all sorts, religious and social, might be held in an informal setting, and the Upper Room was constructed between the choir vestry and the ancient Tower chamber beneath the dusty belfry, because Achdeacon Hopton's "temporary" Church Rooms had been demolished at last. Perhaps all the influences of the many incumbencies are united now in a building which belongs to everyone in Moseley by reason of its age and its many modern functions.

Moseley has changed character not once but twice since the Second World War. In the 1950's many of the remaining wealthier families moved out towards Solihull and the open country. Victorian houses were converted into flats and then many of the smaller ones deteriorated into multi-occupation by often unhappy immigrants. In the 1960's they were joined by the new wave of drug addicts and by many mentally ill people anxious to be close to local hospitals and clinics. Prostitution became a problem in the roads east of the Parade and so Residents Associations were formed in various places to maintain amenities. The modern roads were still attractive to professional and business house buyers and so there were two types of community in Moseley, often living in adjacent roads of widely different character.

Now blocks of modern flats and homes designed for convenience are replacing the crumbling older houses. Practical attempts are being made to solve the social problems of a wider area than Moseley with hostels for various groups, whom many of the community try to support at least with their understanding. The high price of accommodation is drawing stable families back into the area with its solid brick houses and well established gardens. Moseley may have a supermarket but some of the old family businesses are surviving and various attractive new shops have opened. There is even an art gallery in the old stables at the top of Salisbury Road. The Churches and public houses are still significant social centres as some of them have been for centuries. Although threatened, Moseley is still a living and caring community which hopes for a future as varied as its past.

SOURCES USED TO COMPILE THIS HISTORY

In Birmingham Central Reference Library

Survey of Worcestershire-by Thomas Habington
Survey of Worcestershire-by Nash (1781)
Victoria County History - Warwickshire, Worcestershire
Chronological History of Moseley (Notes on past events in Moseley, Balsall Heath, Kings Heath, Kings Norton) by H. J. Everson.
Kings Norton by Lock (1926)
Mainly about Moseley - an introduction to its historical geography by J. M. Jones (1962)
Rambles and Researches among Worcestershire Churches-G. K. Stanton (1896)
W. B. Bickley Collection of newspaper cuttings, miscellaneous M.S.S. and papers re Moseley and Kings Norton
11714-19201
J. Cotton's Collection of cuttings etc. 11866-1924)
The Post Office Directory 1854
Everson's Moseley, Kings Heath and Balsa)) Heath Directory and Year Book 1896
Moseley and Kings Heath Directory 1924
Moseley Society Journal 1894-1909
Birmingham, Moseley and Kings Heath Journal 1909-1933
The Guild of Knowle Register and Transcript by W. B. Bickley
The Grevis Family Papers
Copy of letters patent (Philip and Mary) and revenues of Kings Norton Grammar School and Moseley Chapel

Graves' Memoirs of the Civil War by F.A. Bates (1927)
Collection of Documents on Moseley Hall
Architects' Plans of Moseley Hall and Bordesley Hall
The Taylor Family Papers (1399-1880)
The Inclosure Act for the Parish of Kings Norton 1772
The Inclosure Award for the Parish of Kings Norton
Assessments for Relief of the Poor for the Parish of Kings Norton for 1708, 1787, 1788, 1789, 1798, 1799
Accounts of the Overseers of the Poor for the Parish of Kings Norton for 1774-1777, 1777-1781, 1787-1800, 1803-1837
Relieving Officer's Accounts for the Parish of Kings Norton, 1849
Tithe Map of the Moseley Yield 1840
Tithe Apportionment for the Parish of Kings Norton 1843
Assessments for Property Tax for Moseley Yield in the Parish of Kings Norton for 1813 and 1815
Particulars of the Anderton Park Estate 1877 and map
Plans of 16 areas of Moseley at dates between 1770 and 1885
Warwickshire Photographic Survey 1912 onwards

In Worcester County Record Office

The wills and/or inventories of many Moseley people (1546-1794) as mentioned in the text
Worcestershire Quarter Sessions Records-compiled by Willis Bund
Kings Norton Churchwardens Presentments for 1664, 1684, 1690, 1693, 1699

Public Record Office. London

Will of Richard Grevis, made 1600
Will of Sir Richard Grevis, made 1632
Will of Elizabeth Grevis, made 1654

In Saint Mary's Church, Moseley

Parish Magazines 1907-1970 (Brief history of Moseley by W. J. Spurrier is included in 1908 issues)
Canon Colmore's personal Log Book 1877-1893 (includes cuttings from parish magazines 1879 onwards) vestry Minute Book
Entertainment Committee Minute Book
List of gravestone inscriptions in Moseley Churchyard
Transcript of Moseley Chapel Baptism (1761) and Burial (1762-1850) Registers made by Miss O. M. Horton for the Birmingham and Midland Society for Genealogy and Heraldry
Mr. Sydney Raine's Transcript of Matthew Boulton's Diary and other notes and newspaper cuttings
What to see in Moseley Parish Church-Bax and Chatwin Collection of photographs, paintings and various documents
The building which we know as St. Mary's Parish Church, Moseley, has been known by the following names, variously spelt, over the centuries:- Before the Reformation-the Chapel of Saint Mary, Moseley; the Chapel of Our Lady, Moseley; Moseley Chapel. Mid 16th century to mid 19th century-the Chapel of Moseley or Moseley Chapel. In 1853 the District Chapelry of Moseley was created by Order in Council. In 1866 the building became known as St. Mary's Parish Church, Moseley.

INDEX

Compiling a manageable index has been difficult with so many possible entries. Personal names are listed to assist those interested in family history and some very numerous entries are grouped to save space.

INDEX Continued

PART TWO
Moseley 1970 - 2004

A CHANGING MOSELEY

We were all taught at school or at university that history is about the process of change. What we were not told, but quickly discovered, is that hardly anybody embraces it willingly. As Marshall McLuhan once said, 'We look at the future through rear-view mirrors.'

No more so than in Moseley. Whereas in many of the suburbs of this over-developed city change is likely to offer an improvement on the past, the people of Moseley have long since agreed on what is the perfect version of their 'urban village'. And woe betide anyone who threatens to alter it. The history of Moseley, especially over the last half century, is the history of armed resistance.

The barricades have been staffed (to chose the non-gendered term) pretty well permanently for the last 20 years, and the assaults have come in a variety of forms: road widening, public houses, sheltered accommodation, pigeons, by-passes, rugby supporters, sex clinics, night clubs, property developers, the lack of rugby supporters, fast food outlets and live music. These are a few of our least favourite things.

Such resistance has a long and venerable history. It goes back at least as far as the cutting of Salisbury Road in the late 19th Century, a move that was seen to threaten the tranquillity of the village centre. And one of the reasons that there was never a cinema in Moseley was local disaffection with the idea back in the 1920s. Picture-houses, it was argued, were more appropriate for places like Balsall Heath and Kings Heath. Moseleyites were more than satisfied with a good standard book for the long winter evenings.

What's remarkable - remarkable at least in Birmingham - is the success of many of the campaigns. In 1982, for example, West Midlands County Council scrapped its plan to 'improve' the junction of St Mary's Row and the Alcester Road in the face of sustained local opposition. The plans for a Moseley - Kings Heath by-pass were similarly shelved, though the threat lingered on through much of the 1970s and 1980s. Equally successful was the campaign to close the Gracewell Clinic, the residential unit for sex offenders, which ran from 1988 until 1993.

The 'No more pubs' crusade of the late 1990's succeeded in preventing Bass Taverns (the owners of O'Neil's on the Alcester Road) from expanding its operation into the empty premises next door. And as far back as 1973 the Moseley Tenants' Association was fighting the implications of the City Development Plan for the area. While many of Birmingham's suburbs have embraced re-development as the dual-carriageway to salvation (along with most of the items listed above) in Moseley it has represented the imminent end of civilisation.

Not that opposition has always been triumphant. A drawn-out and painful battle to prevent the arrival of the pub chain, Wetherspoon's, in the village filled meeting-rooms and newspapers throughout 1999 and 2000. This was one battle that Moseley lost. We might add that a number of the most vociferous combatants in that campaign have since been seen drinking there.

It may be that Moseley's single biggest regret in life is that it is not Bournville. In 1999, for example, as work was beginning to transform the centre of Birmingham into an icon of 21st-century shopping, Moseley was reviving its village green, complete with Victorian-style benches and fencing. It was a tradition last seen in that other garden suburb. George Cadbury himself would have watched the move with some satisfaction, though not from the steps of Wetherspoon's.

Chris Upton

THE SOCIO-DEMOGRAPHIC TRAJECTORY OF MOSELEY

Introduction

In this chapter we look at changes in the demographic, ethnic and social class composition of Moseley over the period 1981-2001. Census data is used to compare changes over time. For the purpose of this analysis, 'Moseley' is defined as the Moseley Forum boundary and a 'best fit' of geographical census tracts (i.e. below that of ward level - enumeration districts and Output Areas) was used to aggregate up to the Moseley Forum boundary. This enabled comparison of census data over time. Changes in the questions asked and definitions of variables used in the census meant that the analysis was confined to:

- population change within age-groups (1981-2001)
- ethnicity (1991-2001)
- religion (2001)
- housing tenure (1981-2001)
- number and type of dwellings (2001)
- socio economic group (SEG) (1981-1991) and SEG (re-defined, 2001).

At the end of the chapter we provide a discussion and conclusions.

Demographic trends

From the mid 1970s through to the mid 1990s the Major Urban Areas (MUAs) such as Birmingham, Manchester, Liverpool and Leeds saw their population decline as a result of outward migration to smaller provincial towns and the countryside. This process of 'counter urbanization' is well established in the popular and academic literature and contributed to the decline of inner cities in the core metropolitan areas of conurbations such as the West Midlands. Only recently in Birmingham has there been something of an 'urban renaissance' partly driven by the supply and demand for city centre apartments. This has resulted in a stabilization of population decline with a growth in inner city population between 1991-2001, partly offsetting the continued trend of outward migration from other parts of Birmingham.

In this social climate of 'counter urbanization', suburban neighbourhoods such as Moseley, located close to the 'neglected' inner city of the 1970s and 1980s, should have witnessed a significant decline in population. However, whilst Birmingham's population fell by roughly 40,000 (-4%) between 1981 and 1991, Moseley's population increased by around 300 (+2%). In the next 10 year period (1991-2001), Moseley's population increased by more than 16% (from 15,341 to 17,860), which was substantially greater than the citywide population increase of 2% over the same period. Over the past 20 years therefore, Moseley has gone through its own urban renaissance and witnessed a significant population growth of some 19% compared to a slight reduction in the city's population of around 2% (Table 1)1.

This population increase has occurred across all of the age groups (except 16-24 year olds) at a rate above the average for the city as a whole (Table 1). Significantly, the two age-groups most associated with outward migration (25-44 and 45-59) have increased by more than 31% and 37% respectively compared to a more mixed pattern for Birmingham

Table 1: Demographic profile Moseley and Birmingham, 1981-2001

	1981 No.	1981 %	1991 No.	1991 %	1981-1991 % Change	2001 No.	2001 %	1981-2001% % Change
MOSELEY								
0-4	938	6.2	908	5.9	-3.2	1,062	5.9	+13.2
5-9	813	5.4	928	6.0	14.1	1,115	6.2	+37.1
10-15	1,061	7.1	1,133	7.4	6.8	1,391	7.8	+31.1
16-24	2,907	19.4	2,298	15.0	-20.9	2,354	13.2	-19.0
25-44	4,580	30.5	4,900	31.9	7.0	5,985	33.5	+30.7
45-59	2,171	14.5	2,210	14.4	1.8	2,973	16.6	+36.9
60-74	1,735	11.6	1,673	10.9	-3.6	1,749	9.8	+0.8
75+	810	5.4	1,291	8.4	59.4	1,231	6.9	+52.0
Total pop.	15,015	100	15,341	100	2.2	17,860	100	+18.9
BIRMINGHAM								
0-4	63,685	6.4	73,859	7.7	16.0	69,993	7.2	+9.9
5-9	66,402	6.7	69,524	7.3	4.7	70,953	7.3	+6.9
10-15	100,096	10.1	73,902	7.7	-26.2	88,040	9.0	-12.0
16-24	152,326	15.3	129,251	13.5	-15.1	132,543	13.6	-13.0
25-44	242,445	24.3	265,779	27.8	9.6	276,803	28.3	+14.2
45-59	171,482	17.2	146,045	15.3	-14.8	154,591	15.8	-9.9
60-74	146,637	14.7	134,145	14.0	-8.5	116,154	11.9	-20.8
75+	53,463	5.4	64,130	6.7	20.0	68,155	7.0	+27.5
Total pop.	996,266	100	956635	100	-4.0	977,232	100	-1.9

Table 2 Ethnic minority identity: Birmingham and Moseley, 1991-2001

	MOSELEY 1991	MOSELEY 2001	MOSELEY 1991-2001 absolute change (%)	BIRMINGHAM 1991	BIRMINGHAM 2001	BIRMINGHAM 1991-2001 absolute change (%)
White	74.9	62.8	-4.7	78.5	70.4	-8.8
Black Caribbean	4.1	4.2	16.5	4.7	4.9	6.0
Black African	0.5	1.1	150.1	0.3	0.6	103.4
Black Other	1.0	0.5	-43.1	0.9	0.6	-32.2
Indian	5.3	6.1	30.9	5.3	5.7	9.4
Pakistani	10.1	17.7	99.3	6.9	10.6	56.2
Bangladeshi	0.3	1.2	354.8	1.3	2.1	64.3
Chinese	0.2	1.8	923.3	0.3	1.0	239.0
Mixed	-	3.2	-4.7	-	2.9	-8.8
Base pop.	15,670	17,817	+18.6	960,686	977,057	+2.2

Table 3: Religious affiliation, Birmingham and Moseley, 2001

	MOSELEY No.	MOSELEY %	BIRMINGHAM No.	BIRMINGHAM %
Christian	7,531	45.8	577,783	64.5
Buddhist	129	0.8	3,039	0.3
Hindu	458	2.8	19,359	2.2
Jewish	268	1.6	2,363	0.3
Muslim	3,871	23.6	140,081	15.6
Sikh	492	3.0	28,581	3.2
Other	122	0.7	2,485	0.3
No Religion	3,566	21.7	121,542	13.6
Total	17,882		977,191	

as a whole (+14% and −10% respectively). Overall, the population structure of Moseley is more bunched into the 'working-age' groups (16-59) when compared to the city as a whole and therefore has a lower rate of under 16s and persons of retirement age.

Trends in ethnic profile

But these demographic trends do not tell the full story. The division of Moseley between a relatively prosperous 'south' covering St.Agnes, the Moseley Triangle and the Russells with a more deprived 'north' (to the north of the Moseley Road and centred around Church Road and the area adjacent to Balsall Heath) disguises the underlying dynamics affecting the population structure.

During the mid to late 1980s a young Asian and Black Caribbean population was emerging from the first and second generation of 1950s and 1960s immigrants to Birmingham. These immigrants had settled in parts of Birmingham that had been exposed to the earliest processes of suburbanisation. Council estates built on the city's periphery accepted the white working class, whilst the vacated terraced dwellings of Handsworth, Sparkhill, Sparkbrook, Washwood Heath and Aston led to acute levels of segregation for these immigrants. This has had a profound impact on the demographic structure of the city: in 2001, roughly 30% of the ethnic minority population was under the age of 16 compared to half this rate for the 'white' population. The division of Moseley into a southern 'quarter', less affected by patterns of migration compared to the area adjacent to Balsall Heath, therefore, explains the lower than average population of under 16s in Moseley.

Table 4: Number and % of dwelling types, Birmingham and Moseley, 2001

	MOSELEY		BIRMINGHAM	
	No.	%	No.	%
Detached houses	1,191	14.5	44,444	11.0
Semi detached houses	1,363	16.5	141,147	34.9
Terraced houses	1,468	17.8	126,385	31.3
Purpose built flats	2,233	27.1	72,204	17.9
Converted flats and bedsits	1,905	23.1	15,628	3.9
Commercial flats	79	1.0	4,317	1.1
Mobile homes/caravans	3	>0.1	149	>0.1
Total	**8,242**	**100**	**404,274**	**100**
Vacant dwellings	386	4.9	12933	3.3

Table 5: Household tenure, Birmingham and Moseley, 1981-2001

	MOSELEY			BIRMINGHAM		
	1981	1991	2001	1981	1991	2001
Owner Occupiers	47.0	51.3	53.1	52.6	60.1	60.4
Social Rented Housing	19.7	24.2	23.2	38.7	32.0	27.7
Council Housing	5.5	4.9	5.6	34.7	26.4	19.4
Housing Association	14.2	19.3	17.6	4.0	5.6	8.3
Privately Renting	33.2	24.5	23.6	8.7	7.9	11.8
Employment	0.9	1.0		1.0	1.3	
Unfurnished	10.6	6.5		4.7	3.3	
Furnished	21.7	17.0		3.0	3.4	
Base (No. of households)	6,395	6,873	7,841	356,733	374,037	390,775

Nevertheless, Moseley has and continues to support a more diverse population than Birmingham. In 1981, 25% of its population had been born outside England compared to 18% for the city as a whole; by 2001 successive generations of immigrants' children meant that the proportion born outside England was roughly similar to that in 1981. However, analysis of 'country of birth' is partly irrelevant in the context of second and third generation of 1950s and 1960s immigration. In 1991 the population census included for the first time a question on ethnic identity. This revealed that Moseley had a larger ethnic minority population relative to Birmingham whilst the combined Indian, Pakistani and Bangladeshi population made up more than 15% of the population − greater than for the city as a whole (Table 2).

Between 1991 and 2001, Moseley's ethnic minority population (non-white) increased by almost 70% and continued to exceed the proportion for Birmingham as a whole (Table 2). The most significant trend in the intervening period between 1991 and 2001 has been the growth of the Pakistani population, which has almost doubled in Moseley and represents almost 18% of the population compared to just under 11% across Birmingham.

The diversity of Moseley is also reflected in the range of faiths practiced (a theme picked up later in this book). The 2001 census was the first census to ask a question of religious affiliation. The results in Table 3 show that the practice of Islam is at a rate in excess of the proportion of the population from Islamic countries identified in the 'ethnicity' tables from the Census (e.g. Pakistan and Bangladesh). This may reflect differences in the way individuals identify their religious affiliation as opposed to their ethnic association. More probable is that the higher than average proportion of the population affiliated to the Islamic faith reflects the trend in asylum seeker and refugee migration from the Middle East (especially from Iran and Iraq) that has moved into Moseley. As a consequence, almost 25% of Moseley's population identified with Islam compared to around 16% of Birmingham's total population.

Given the trends in ethnicity and demographic change, Christianity appears to be in significant decline, with less than 50% of the population identifying themselves as Christians. Moseley, consequently, is more pluralist in its religious outlook with a higher than average representation of Buddhists, Sikhs and Jews as well as a significant proportion of the population expressing no religious belief (22% compared to 14% citywide).

Housing choices

Moseley's population increase and its ethnic and religious diversity reflect flexibility in housing choices (the size and style of dwellings available), proximity (to local and city centre services), the value stored in the wealth of heritage and a historic tolerance to different lifestyles and backgrounds. In 2003, Birmingham City Council's Housing Department conducted a survey to establish to which parts of the city people aspire. The results from the survey revealed that more than two-thirds of the ethnic minority population living outside Moseley said they would prefer to live here and the evidence above suggests that a diverse population increasingly chooses to live in Moseley.

The 'flexibility' of Moseley to meet different household needs and lifestyle arrangements is reflected in a more 'balanced' provision of dwelling types and housing tenures than compared to the city as a whole. Less than a third of Moseley's housing stock is of terraced or semi-detached construction compared to more than two-thirds of Birmingham's; it has a slightly higher provision of detached properties and more than 50% of Moseley's housing stock is classified as flats or bed-sits compared to 22% of Birmingham's total stock (Table 4).

The ownership of housing in Moseley (housing tenure) is also more balanced: roughly a 50:50 split between owner occupation and rented housing compared to a 60:40 split across Birmingham in 2001. The profile of housing tenure has changed somewhat over the past 20 years with a decline in private rented accommodation and an increase in social renting (council and housing association provision). The trend in private renting is against the city trend which saw an increase from 9% to almost 12% (partly fuelled by an increase in city living and city centre developments including the buy-to-let market) between 1981-2001. However, with almost a quarter of Moseley residents in private rented housing, the proportion in Moseley is well in excess of the national or city average. The increase in social rented accommodation is against the national and citywide trends; the city, for example, saw a decline in social renting from 39% to 28% whilst Moseley's share rose from just under 20% to 23%.

In summary, between 1981 and 2001, owner occupation in Moseley increased by 39% (+26% for Birmingham), social renting increased by 44% (-22%) and private renting provision decreased by 13% (+49% across Birmingham). These trends in rented accommodation provision indicate a 'regulation' of the rented market (with more involvement from the state and quasi-state sector) and a decline in furnished accommodation for the 'student' market.

Table 6: Socio-Economic Group, Birmingham and Moseley, 2001	MOSELEY (2001)	BIRMINGHAM (2001)
Employers and professional	43.7	25.6
Employers (large establishments) and higher managerial	3.5	2.7
Higher professional occupations	13.7	5.1
Lower managerial and professional	26.5	17.8
Non-Manual	18.8	24.0
Intermediate occupations	8.8	10.3
Small employers/own account workers	6.0	5.8
Lower supervisory and technical occupations	4.0	7.9
Semi routine/routine work	13.7	26.9
Never worked or LT unemployed	13.4	11.2
F/T students	10.9	12.2
Base (No.)	11,340	561,272

Table 7: Socio-Economic Group, Birmingham and Moseley, 1981-1991	MOSELEY 1981	MOSELEY 1991	BIRMINGHAM 1981	BIRMINGHAM 1991
Employers and professional 'class'	23.6	26.2	8.0	11.3
Employers & Manager in large establishments	4.6	4.0	3.3	4.4
Employers & Managers in small establishments	8.3	11.8	5.6	7.4
Professional self-employed	1.2	2.0	0.5	0.9
Professional employee	8.8	13.6	2.5	3.8
Artists and craft related occupations	23.6	26.2	8.0	11.3
Non-Manual occupations	24.6	18	26.5	27.4
Foremen and Supervisors Non-Manual	1.8	0.7	1.1	1.1
Junior Non-Manual	19.6	14.3	19.8	21.0
Personal Service Workers	3.2	3.0	5.6	5.3
Manual occupations	24.3	18.3	50.4	39.5
Foremen and Supervisors Manual	0.6	1.0	2.8	2.2
Skilled manual	9.4	6.9	20.7	16.2
Semi-skilled Manual	9.4	8.4	19.3	15.2
Unskilled Manual	4.9	2.0	7.6	5.9
Other	4.7	5.9	3.4	5.4
Base (No.)	852	692	50,134	38,638

Social Class

The decline in the 'student' housing market reflects a lower than average student population, This is confirmed by analysis of the demographic and social class position of Moseley and Birmingham. As Table 1 shows, Moseley's 16-24 age-group was the only age-group to see a decline in absolute terms. Whilst this is a trend in line with what occurred across Birmingham, the relative decline is sharper: -19% compared to -13%. As a result, the proportion of the population in Moseley that was classified as a full-time student at the time of the 2001 census was below the average for Birmingham (Table 6).

A change in the way social class is recorded in the census precludes straight comparison of 2001 with 1981-1991. At the time of the 2001 census, almost half of Moseley's working-age population was classified as in the

Professional/Employer class (Table 6) - almost double the rate for Birmingham. Between 1981 and 1991, this class increased across the city relative to other groups, however, the rate in Moseley was more than double the Birmingham rate. Significantly, given the symbolism of Moseley as a 'Bohemian' neighbourhood, more than a quarter of the working age population was employed in art or craft related professions. Finally, a decline in manual occupations across the city is also evident in Moseley, however, the higher than average proportion of people either long-term unemployed or 'never worked' points to a polarised occupational structure within Moseley.

Conclusion and discussion

Clearly, Moseley has a diverse population that has changed significantly over the past 20 years. Against national and citywide trends, Moseley's population has increased and changed in ways that would not have been expected in the late 1970s. Its demographic profile has become more ethnically diverse and is more likely to be of working age and whilst Moseley has continued to house a professional and artistic class, which has increased, it is also polarised with a larger proportion of long-term unemployed. This trend together with the decline in student numbers reflects changes in the structure of the rented housing market. Greater 'regulation' of the rented sector - reflected in an increase in social rented housing – allows more housing options for economically marginal groups. At the same time, increased provision of owner occupation, through new build and de-conversion of larger multiply-occupied housing, fuelled by above average increases in house prices, has catered for the growing professional class.

Moseley's 'success' is a reflection of the structure of housing and urban environmental provision laid down in the 19th century, which has proved to be enduringly popular and flexible. Its popularity is reflected in the change and the growth in Moseley's population over recent times, whilst its flexibility as a neighbourhood, catering for diverse lifestyles and housing arrangements, is reflected in the range of housing choices available which serve a variety of households' needs. Planned at different density levels around a local centre with amenities and services close to hand, the popularity of Moseley is enduring. In this way demographic and social change within Moseley is inextricably linked to what housing is on offer: the range of styles and types of housing that enable people to make the housing choices necessary at different stages of their lives and allows households to progress through different dwelling types (flats, terraced, detached properties) and ownership arrangements (private and social renting and home ownership).

However, the continued polarization of the housing market between high price owner occupation and a regulated social rented sector has resulted in a decline in a more transient student population. As noted above, only one age-group has seen a relative and absolute population decrease: the 16-24 age group. This indicates that Moseley's student population has declined through a process of 'professionalisation' and gentrification of the housing market. This is a concern as it reduces the pool of talent and mindsets that contributes to the diversity of Moseley as a symbol of alternative lifestyles.

Moseley will continue to prosper as its diversity of housing, the quality of its environment and its proximity to the city centre will continue to advantage it over other neighbourhoods. Its distinctive feature is its 'Bohemian' character, which contributes to a tolerance of diversity that needs to be retained in a post-September 11th 2001 environment. Moseley together with Sparkhill contributes to one of the largest concentrations of the Pakistani/Bangladeshi population outside London - whilst Moseley's Islamic population is second only to a declining Christian population. Radicalism and the replenishment of ideas are important as counterpoints to conservative values that can undermine tolerance and diversity.

Peter Lee

PART 1 : MOSELEY STRUCTURES

ARCHITECTURE

Woodbridge Road - the old Milk Depot site

In the thirty or so years that constitute the end of the twentieth century the buildings of Moseley changed little. Many of the Victorian and Edwardian structures remain intact, and where there has been new development, it has often been in a style that pays homage to its older brethren. Whilst this is a compliment to the earlier designers, it creates little more than a pastiche, and even this has not always been done well. This is somewhat sad within a community brimming with creative minds.

Perhaps the most significant architectural influence has been the designation of two Conservation Areas. These are defined as areas of special architectural or historic interest, the character and appearance of which it is desirable to preserve or enhance. The first designation was in 1983. It included the main shopping centre and a number of nearby residential roads. A second Area, around St Agnes church, followed in 1987. Within these Areas, development is subject to stricter Town Planning controls, and Listed Building consent is usually required. Developers are encouraged to refurbish rather than demolish.

The eighties saw a great deal of social housing. Most of this was carried out by housing associations and has a commonality of style and materials characteristic of this type of development. These buildings have been carried out within tight budgets and tend to be rather bland in appearance. Just off the Wake Green Road there is one notable exception. It is the delightful scheme produced for Lenches' Trust by the architects S T Walker and Partners. This was completed in 1983 and received a Housing Design Award.

In the late nineties the housing market boomed. In particular there was an increased demand for smart apartments. Whilst this was partly a life-style phenomenon, it was also a response to the buy-to-let market. Buildings such as the Midland Counties Milk depot in Woodbridge Road, the Sorrento Hospital and the Britannic Insurance offices at Moor Green Lane have been redeveloped for residential use.

Private housing and apartments have replaced the student accommodation at Gracie Hall, and even the once hallowed Reddings rugby football ground has succumbed to the trend. An interesting example of new residential building appears on land adjacent to the Village public house. Designed by the architects Brophy Associates, it provides live-work accommodation built in a modern idiom.

The growing leisure market has spawned a host of new pubs and restaurants within the village centre. The Moseley Gentlemen's Club is now the Village Public House, Gascoignes furniture store the Elizabeth of York, and TSB bank the Salisbury. There are several other new drinking venues and a scattering of restaurants. Falling within the jurisdiction of the Conservation Area, these refurbishments have helped preserve the original architecture, but, sadly, have done little to enhance it. As with the house builders, the brewers trudge along the pastiche path to mediocrity, although the Cross wine bar and the Bulls Head pub provide a glimmer of hope. With a number of notable exceptions, the quality of shop fronts has not seen the improvement that might have been expected within a Conservation Area.

On the more positive side, the Moseley Society, formed in 1979, has been influential in preserving and enhancing the area. In particular the decaying dovecote in the grounds of Moseley Hall has been restored and regularly opened to visitors. Similar restoration work has been done to the icehouse in the private park. The village 'green' has undergone cosmetic surgery and now provides a much more attractive and usable space. It gives a focus to the village, and provides a home for the monthly farmers' market.

Let us hope that the future architecture of Moseley is created with proper respect for the past but with an honesty that acknowledges its place in the twenty-first century.

Ken Fisher

MOSELEY STRUCTURES

ELECTORAL BOUNDARIES

An important characteristic of a community in a city such as Birmingham is that it has a strong political voice. Moseley has a long history of political involvement and has consistently had one of the city's highest voting electorates. It was therefore surprising that for many years Moseley did not have a concerted political voice within Birmingham. The electoral wards which make up Birmingham are set by the Boundary Commission for England, a statutory committee of The Electoral Commission. The Electoral Committee is an independent body established by the Political Parties, Elections and Referendums Act 2000 which took over the functions of the Local Government Commission for England. This body and its predecessors have determined the political boundaries within major cities such as Birmingham for many years.

In 1962 The Boundary Commission established a City Council comprising 42 wards, one of which was called Moseley and was made up of most of the area recognised as Moseley. It was The Boundary Commission review of 1979 that

The heavy line shows the new boundary of the Ward. The thinner line to the north and the east shows the old boundaries

radically altered Moseley by establishing a Moseley and Kings Heath ward. In addition to abolishing the previous Moseley ward, the new Moseley and Kings Heath ward did not even contain all of Moseley, with the boundary being drawn along the middle of Alcester Road from Brighton Road to the traffic lights at the junction with Salisbury Road, then passing up St Mary's Row and along Wake Green Road. The consequence of this was that the whole of the northern part of Moseley was moved into the Sparkhill ward, with the remainder of Moseley being part of a larger ward which was dominated by Kings Heath.

The reasons for this division are not fully clear, however the proposals put to the Boundary Commission by the Labour Party in May 1977 proposed something similar. It was also apparent that the people of Moseley failed to recognise the importance of responding to the Boundary Commission at an early enough stage. The Commission had publicised its review in 1975, but it was only once the proposals were published that the community responded. However, these objections were not heeded.

Consequently, Moseley's ability to respond to issues as a community suffered, much to the annoyance of the community. The absurdity of this continued to be highlighted by the growing identity of Moseley as a 'village community'. The local Moseley and Kings Heath and Sparkhill councillors attempted to respond to Moseley issues, but it was clearly difficult for the two groups to focus upon Moseley issues when they had additional issues to respond to in their wards. This unfortunate state of affairs was partially alleviated by the establishment of the Central Moseley Neighbourhood Forum which provided a unifying voice for the Moseley community. One of the first decisions of the Forum was to campaign for a change in the Ward boundaries. As a result, the community was prepared when the Local Government Commission for England initiated a periodic review of Birmingham's electoral boundaries in December 2001. Each of the major political parties made proposals to the Commission and the Forum presented a submission which had been agreed at a well attended public meeting. Following consultations, The Boundary Commission reported to the Electoral Commission in May 2003 and recommended an increase in the number of Birmingham's electoral wards from 39 to 40; they also redrew almost all the existing boundaries. Happily for Moseley, this put most of Northern Moseley back into the ward, which also gained a small part of the old Bournville ward; other parts of the old Moseley and Kings Heath ward were transferred to the new Sparkbrook and Springfield wards. Whilst this did not fully correspond to the Forum's proposals, Moseley is now politically one unit again; the June 2004 elections were contested using the new boundaries, with the ward returning the highest proportion of the vote as usual. We now look forward to our councillors being more able to respond to the needs of the Moseley community.

Michael Wakelam

MOSELEY STRUCTURES

THE MOSELEY SOCIETY

1979
Inaugural meeting May. In response to plans for road widening at the Moseley crossroads, the disgusting state of the public car park and the inappropriate design of the then new Tesco supermarket. 34 present. Committee set up and Aims of Society stated:-
- Non-political
- Preservation and protection
- Development and improvement
- Represent opinion on matters of general interest

Resolved to initiate a car park clean-up scheme and to oppose the road widening plans.

1979 – 1980
Started to monitor planning applications.
Successfully opposed road widening.
Regular car park clean-ups established.

1980 - 1981
Adopted amended constitution suggested by Civic Trust to allow Registration and to seek charitable status.

1981 - 1982
Initiation of dovecote restoration programme.
Acceptance of proposal by Chantry Road and Park Hill Residents' Association for establishment of a Moseley Conservation Area.

1982 – 1983
Success in preventing road widening proposals.
Licence to restore Dovecote granted.

1983 - 1984
Start of oral history group (later to become Moseley Local History Society).

1985 – 1986
Opening of restored Dovecote.
Abandonment of 'Improvement Lines' (road widening).
Formation of Local History Society.

1986 - 1987
Regular public openings of Dovecote and 'Cow house'.

1987 - 1988
Threat of tunnel under or by-pass of Kings Heath with road along railway cutting through Moseley as a link with the M40 (opposed).

1988 - 1989
Publication of the booklet of *Moseley's Listed Buildings*.

1990 – 1991
Publication of *Moseley Personalities*.
Publication of *History of Moseley Hall (jointly)*.

1991 - 1992
Success opposing latest proposal for road widening.
Production of Design Guide for Shopfronts in Moseley by City.
Revised Moseley Action Plan as part of the Unitary Development Plan.
Establishment of bottle banks in car park for recycling glass.
Publication of *History of Presbyterian Church*

1992 – 1993
Establishment of Area of Restraint for institutional properties.
Publication of Moseley Architectural poster.

1993 - 1994
Publication of second volume of *Moseley Personalities*.
Introduction of all-red phase for pedestrian crossings at crossroads.

1995 - 1996
Recognition by 'The Tidy Britain Group' which presented a certificate for Good work in the car park.
Society mentioned in The Queen Mother's birthday Awards.

1996 – 1997
Presentation of Award for Voluntary Organisations as part of The Queen Mother's Birthday Awards 1996.
Launch of public appeal for funds to restore the ice house and to create a wildlife garden at the Dovecote.
Creation of The Moseley Society web page.

1997 - 1998
Establishment of Central Moseley Neighbourhood Forum.

1998 – 1999
Restoration of Ice House in Moseley Park Booklet to accompany Moseley Trail as part of Heritage Open Days.

1999 - 2000
Village Green refurbishment.
Formal opening of restored Ice House by Chris Upton and public open days started.
New wooden staircase in Cow house.

2000 - 2001
Establishment of Moseley Community Development Trust.

2001 – 2002
Publication of *'The Great Walls of Moseley'* as guidelines for domestic enclosures.
Purchase of old Post Office building as home of Moseley Community Development Trust.
Appointment of street wardens.

2002 – 2003
Final plans for '18th C period garden' sustaining wildlife approved for Dovecote area.

Planning

Since the registration of the Society as the Civic Trust registered 'Amenity Society' for Moseley, the City's Planning Department has given us notice of significant planning applications in the area. We are fortunate that residents with architectural and town planning skills have always been represented on the Committee and have examined plans, supporting or lodging objections as appropriate to meet the Society's published policy.

Planning Guidance was included in the Unitary Development Plan. It has had a significant effect on the area, preventing further sub-division of properties for multiple occupation, or into new institutional uses.

The Society was closely involved in the production of the Moseley Action Plan and the Moseley Village Non Retail Uses Policy, both also adopted as Supplementary Planning Guidance.

The Society is represented on the Conservation Areas Advisory committee, and volunteers have recently helped draft Appraisal and Character Statements for both the Moseley and St Agnes Conservation Areas.

Fiona Adams and Roy Cockel

MOSELEY STRUCTURES

MOSELEY FORUM

During the 1990's one local government priority was to involve people in decision-making to a greater extent. This was achieved in a number of different ways, one of which in Birmingham was the establishment of Neighbourhood Forums.

Here in Moseley, this coincided with local concern about the shopping centre, which was brought to a head when the former Tesco store moved out. There had been real worries about the viability of Moseley as a retail centre, and about the signs of decay and lack of investment in the environment. A Moseley Action Plan was initiated, mostly because of effective pressure applied by the Moseley Society. In the early 90's, representatives of City Council departments (chiefly Planning and Transportation) met with representatives of the Moseley Society and other concerned bodies and residents on a regular basis to draw up and then implement the Moseley Action Plan. The Action Plan formed part of the Supplementary Planning Guidance to be taken into account when the Council was considering planning applications for the area. The main direct benefits of the Plan were environmental improvements to Victoria Parade, the car park and the village green.

Terry Lovell
Moseley Forum

When the Action Plan group met, an officer of the Council would often be invited to the meeting to explain his or her own role or that of his/her department so that possible benefits to Moseley could be explored. One such officer was Martin Tolman who was responsible for supporting Neighbourhood Forums in the City. Neighbourhood Forums had been established in 1991 to give citizens a greater say in local matters. As a result of hearing the benefits of Neighbourhood Forums, the group decided to see if the people of Moseley would like to have one here.

Pam Rutter

There was a process to be followed: a petition had to be signed by residents, requesting a public meeting. The meeting had to be attended by at least 20 people, after which a steering group was set up and the Central Moseley Neighbourhood Forum was launched in 1998.

Since then, our Moseley Forum has gone from strength to strength. Its best known activity is probably the monthly Farmers' Market, recently voted the best in the West Midlands. The Forum also worked hard to get sensible new boundaries for Moseley Ward drawn up in the latest review by the Boundary Commission. Very recently, the main thrust of the Forum work has been a 'Planning for Real' exercise in which a large 3D map of Moseley has been constructed and taken to school fetes, Farmers' Markets and the like so that the views of local people can be sought as to which issues need to be addressed in the forthcoming Moseley Community Plan. Another achievement of which the Forum is very proud is that the Moseley Community Development Trust was set up by cooperation between the Forum and the Moseley Society; part of the constitution of the CDT is that there will be 2 representatives of the Forum on its Board, so the link will continue.

The Forum has a management committee of 15 which meets monthly. Several times a year, public meetings are organised. Topics have included: hustings for the local government elections, GM foods, the Alcohol Free Zone and transport issues.

Moseley Forum is affiliated to the Birmingham Association of Neighbourhood Forums (BANF), which now consists of about 80 Forums. BANF's vision is that Birmingham will be a City of flourishing neighbourhoods. Moseley is often cited informally as one such flourishing neighbourhood and it is groups like the Forum that have encouraged community life and active citizenship in recent years.

Pam Rutter

MOSELEY STRUCTURES

THE COMMUNITY DEVELOPMENT TRUST

Fiona Adams

In 1998 the Forum had been born, with a committee of new, young community representatives. Peter Lee was the first Chairman, and often in response to questions about difficult-to-tackle issues at public meetings he would say 'what Moseley needs is a Community Development Trust'.

On a personal level, having been a 'home teacher' for a woman from the Pakistani community in North Moseley since 1976, I was becoming increasingly aware of the difficulties her children, and their peer groups, were having in finding decent, adequately remunerated employment.

The result of these and other influences was the decision to set up a Community Development Trust and another Steering Group, drawn from the Society and the Forum Committees. Various 'local experts' were invited to Steering Group meetings, and Andrew Matheson of Moseley and District Churches Housing Association joined the group, as did an assistant director from the Economic Development Department, then living in Wake Green Road.

The Moseley Society and Forum Committee had a joint meeting and were asked to suggest what they thought the new Trust should do – there was overwhelming support for the idea of opening an information and resources centre in one of the empty shops. It would be the first (and only) public building in Moseley, and would provide some of the information available elsewhere in libraries and Neighbourhood Offices. It would be a meeting point where all members of Moseley's diverse community could meet on equal terms, and where integration could lead to innovation.

In order to get the process going, a charitable trust made an initial grant to pay for a feasibility study, and then offered three years of funding to employ staff and start the process off. Moseley and District Churches Housing Association handled the grants and enabled the Steering Group to advertise for a Development Officer. Tony Thapar was appointed in 2000 as a temporary MDCHA employee, and his first job was to set up the CDT as a company, and employer. The CDT was registered as a Company on 20th February 2001.

All the empty shop properties were investigated with particular interest being taken in the former WH Smith shop. In the end, the decision to purchase the Post Office building was taken quickly, and a charitable trust agreed to make a grant sufficient to buy the freehold. The building became ours on 1st October 2001 – and before long we were dealing with floods from inadequate drains, an unreliable boiler, the need for a burglar alarm, and a request to site a mobile mast on the roof.

The Development Trust now employs three full time staff – its Development Co-ordinator and two administrators, a part-time volunteer co-ordinator and two part-time Street Wardens. It has opened an Information Centre, staffed by volunteers, and its building provides offices leased to local charities and meeting spaces for a wide variety of groups, as well as having the Post Office as its tenant. It supports the Moseley Forum – especially in their efforts to run the award-winning Farmers' Market. Discussions are under way about how the many creative people who live in Moseley can be helped to grow businesses locally and thus contribute to local regeneration.

Those of us involved regard the Community Development Trust as the most hopeful new venture in Moseley for many years. At last we have paid staff to support the voluntary work that has been one of the hallmarks of the area. We have a public building - a first for Moseley. Until now the only publicly owned building in the centre of Moseley was the police station in Woodbridge Road, which is now closed to the public, and the public lavatories in the car park - also under threat of closure. The staff and trustees are now working on ways to ensure the Development Trust can ensure its long term viability, through rental income from the Post Office building, and other ventures in the pipeline.

Fiona Adams

MOSELEY STRUCTURES

LOCAL POLITICS

On May 11th 1911, the Greater Birmingham Bill was passed by Parliament and most of Birmingham's modern boundaries were then established. Moseley was truly incorporated into the city, the electoral ward being called Moseley & Kings Heath. Such was the Conservative dominance between 1912 and 1949 that out of the 30 elections taking place in this period, on 16 occasions Conservatives were elected unopposed. Where there were contests, the only party that consistently challenged the Tories was the Labour party. Until 1960 on only two occasions did a third party join in, the Liberals contesting the seats in 1945 and 1946.

Between 1912 and 1970, the Conservatives obtained on average between 70 and 80 percent of the votes. Labour was generally in second place, but with only 20 - 30% of the votes, was effectively fighting an uphill struggle. Only in 1945 was there a close fought election in Moseley, but even then the Conservative margin of victory was more than 10%. Between 1961 and 1963, the Liberal vote was higher than Labour but was still a long way short of beating the incumbent Tories. Their share of the vote then declined, putting them behind Labour.

In 1970, the Conservative vote showed the first signs of decline, dropping to just over 64%; thereafter there followed a slow but perceptible weakening in their support. The Labour vote started a slow but significant climb. In 1980, the Conservative vote dropped below 50% for the first time, with their majority being below 1000. In 1984, the Conservatives were re-elected with a majority of only 23. In 1986, Eve Brook became the first Labour councillor for the ward with 45% of the vote compared to 33% for the Tories. In 1987, David Hickman held the seat for the Conservatives, but in 1988, John Anderson became the second Labour councillor. In 1990, Eve Brook was re-elected with a large majority and in 1991, Andy Howell was elected to give Labour a clean sweep. In 1992, Ken Hardeman regained the seat for the Tories but lost it to Bryan Nott in 1996.

From 1996, the Labour seats were closely fought with majorities being consistently less than 1000. In 2004, there was a major boundary revision. There was a general election for the whole Council with three Councillors being elected for each ward. Moseley returned 1 Labour and 2 Liberal Democrat councillors.

Eve Brooke
The first Labour councillor for Moseley

Anthony Beaumont Dark
MP for Selly Oak
1979 - 1992

Who were the voters?

The ward electorate has changed dramatically in size over the years. In 1911, there were only 5054 electors for Moseley and Kings Heath. Until 1918, those entitled to vote were restricted to ratepayers who occupied a building of any value or land with a yearly value of £10. Married women did not enjoy the same voting rights as men. Although their husband was entitled to vote on the basis of the property they lived in, wives did not have the same entitlement to the vote.

In 1918, the franchise was extended to men over 21 who were tenants of land or premises, provided that they had been resident for not less than 6 months. Lodgers were only entitled to vote if their rooms were let to them unfurnished. Women over 21 were entitled to vote only if the condition of their employment would have entitled them to vote if they were men. From 1918, married women over 30 could now vote if they resided in a property that entitled their husband to vote.

By 1919 the electorate of Moseley and Kings Heath had risen to 12,877. In 1927, it had grown by a further third to 16441. Until the second World War it remained between 18,000 and 20,000. By 1947, it had grown to 35,122. In 1950, there were boundary changes which reduced the electorate to just under 22000. There were further boundary changes in 1962, 1973, 1982 and 2004. The electorate has remained between 17000 and 20000 since 1962.

Over the years, a higher proportion of Moseley residents have generally turned out to vote in local elections than in many other wards. Between 1911 and 2004 there were only four occasions when the percentage turnout fell below 30%. For most of the time, the turnout has varied between the mid-thirties and mid-forties. There have been many occasions when the turnout has exceeded 50%, the highest being in 1979 when it reached 68.55%.

Michael Wolffe

MOSELEY STRUCTURES

EDUCATION

Moseley School, now Spring Hill Sixth Form College

As Moseley grew as a popular residental area so the provision for State education increased.

There are now seven Primary schools, five of them religious based: St Mary's (Church of England), St Monica's, St Bernard's, and St Martin de Porres (Roman Catholic) and King David's (Jewish). Park Hill and Moor Green are run by the Council. St Mary's, which had moved from the old building founded by Dean Hook to a modern building on the site of the old Vicarage, continues to select pupils according to their Anglican belief, but the Catholic Schools, established to cater for the families of Irish immigrants who had come to Birmingham seeking employment, have suffered from falling rolls. This was because over the years these families had moved on or returned to Ireland. When the British Empire collapsed, and the inhabitants of former colonies were granted British citizenship, many of them came to Britain to look for work in manufacturing towns such as Birmingham. They valued the religious bias of education, even though it was not always their own religion, and took the vacant places in these and the Jewish school, which welcomed them from nearby districts. They blended in very happily, and so these Moseley schools took on the character of the rest of Birmingham as a multicultural area, with pupils from all over the world. Thus it was that falling birthrate in other areas, which had meant closure of some schools, did not affect Moseley.

Many of these pupils hoped to pass the entrance examination for one of the five King Edward Foundation Grammar Schools of Birmingham, which still retained their Grammar School status, and many succeeded. Most Grammar Schools had now become Comprehensive, under the Labour Government in 1968. Many of the new Comprehensive Schools struggled to fulfil their promised role and people thought more highly of the old Grammar Schools, so much so that people moved into the area in the hope of gaining a place for their children in one.

Moseley Grammar School for Boys was not one of the Foundation however, so in 1974, it was united with Moseley Modern School to become a Comprehensive mixed school, providing a wide range of subjects up to A-level. Although this was quite a culture shock for both schools, the amalgamation went smoothly. The school became popular with many of those immigrants who came to Birmingham and prides itself on its rich ethnic diversity, cultural, religious and linguistic. It won a Charter Mark for Excellence, a School Achievement Award, and specialises as a Language College. Several of its pupils have won sports awards as well. However the distinguished Victorian building of the Grammar School, one of Birmingham's architectural landmarks, was found to be crumbling and unsafe and in need of expensive repairs, beyond the compass of the Education Authority. A magnificent effort by the headmistress Mrs Mary Miles and her staff secured grants from the Heritage Lottery Fund, the European Regional Development Fund, and Birmingham City Council, totalling four million, six hundred thousand pounds. The wonderfully restored building then became Spring Hill Sixth Form College, with facilities for education in the Community, a tribute to its original status as a Theological College. The Heritage Lottery Fund also provided a Health and Fitness Centre to share with the Community.

Meanwhile, Queensbridge Secondary Modern School, also mixed, on the southern boundary, became Comprehensive, providing secondary education up to age sixteen. This too has a rich ethnic mix of pupils, and has been recognised by the Department of Education as a High Value School and granted a School Achievement Award. It has been designated as Birmingham's first Arts College, which creates opportunities in Performing Arts, such as Drama, Music and Dance. Liason with professional bodies results in high quality productions and motivates and inspires the pupils, some of whom go on to a career in the Arts.

Fox Hollies Special School has been relocated to the site with a brand new building and shares many of the facilities, including the Creative Arts Suite. There are also four new Science Labs, a new Computer Room with 70 computers, plus a learning Support Centre. Both the secondary schools also run classes in Further Education with a wide range of courses.

All these impressive facilities reflect a large investment in Education in Moseley which flourishes, not only as a valuable asset to the local community, but to the well-being and progress of the city as a whole.

Pam Laslett

PART TWO : RELIGIONS

ST MARY'S PARISH CHURCH

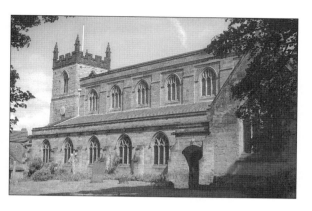

In 1973, when Lorys Davies was Vicar, St Mary's embarked on a project that was to pre-occupy it for over 30 years. A few years earlier, the old vicarage had been demolished and a modern vicarage built in a corner of the grounds. A modern church primary school was built on the larger part of the old vicarage plot and the old National School, dating from the 1820's, had all but closed to active teaching. The deeds of the National School showed that if it ever ceased to be used as a school the freehold of the site would revert to the church for the service of the community. Accordingly, an opportunity arose for the development of a community centre. The inadequate parish hall, affectionately known as the 'Tin Tabernacle', still stood in the grounds of the vicarage, and this was demolished. The dramatically enlarged old school premises became available for parish functions, as well as providing facilities for a plethora of clubs, groups and societies, and meaningful community support activities. With funding from Birmingham City Council and other charities, these community support activities formed the 'raison d'etre' of St Mary's Youth and Community Centre known as 'Centre 13'. It assumed the identity not only of a church initiative but also of a secular community project, and this enhanced its acceptability to the wide range of users it attracted so successfully. The dual identity of Centre 13 was an essential feature of St Mary's outreach to the socially and ethnically mixed local community.

Sadly, in 2004, Centre 13 closed, having become financially unviable as a result of the gradual withdrawal of external funding: but that is another story. Meanwhile, the parish church itself was engaged in managing and embracing change in its regular activities and the facilities of the church itself.

St Mary's church is a late Victorian/Edwardian enlargement of a nicely proportioned building dating from the early 1800's. It has been described as having a grotesquely enlarged nave that is quite out of keeping against its 15th century tower. The reason for this is obvious considered against the practical needs of accommodating a burgeoning congregation. Indeed, inside the enlarged nave there was even a first floor gallery, now long since removed without trace. Ironically, within a few generations of having enlarged the building and almost doubling its seating capacity, there began a reduction in congregations generally to the extent that the building is not now filled to capacity except for a handful of services a year at Easter and Christmas. However, the Christingle children's service early on Christmas Eve now attracts over 500 people, and has done so regularly over the past 30 years, with the exception of a period after the terrorist bombing of the Birmingham Rotunda.

Facilities in and around the building are and always have been, severely restricted. At the beginning of this period, a first floor was added above the choir vestry for meetings of the parochial church council and for Sunday school teaching. The severely cramped vicar's office was moved out of church into the first floor of one of the buildings that front onto St Mary's row, and a door knocked through the side wall facing the main church entrance. At this time a 'Good As New' shop, the profits from which were donated exclusively to Centre 13, occupied the ground floor, and the church's full time verger occupied a flat on the second floor. When the verger retired, the flat was used as additional Sunday school teaching space. The need for income eventually dictated that the second floor was rented out as commercial premises and, for many years, it has been occupied happily by Abbey Candles, who supply traditional candles to a wide variety of churches and other customers.

Before 1969, the font was in the bay under the tower, in what was a well-proportioned baptistry. However, with the reduction in congregations it was apparent that some pews might usefully be removed at the rear of the north aisle to provide a lounge area. The font was moved in 1969 to a central position in this new north aisle lounge, and to facilitate personal counselling a fine modern screen enclosed the bay under the tower.

Around 1980, the church bells needed attention as over the years the spindles on which they pivot had severely corroded and there was a risk of collapse. They had not been rung since the ringing floor was removed to expose the full height of the west window from the nave, and the floor above the west window did not provide sufficient height for ringing from that position. With the assistance of ringers from Yardley parish church, the bells were re-hung, and now provide a unique peel of eight cast steel bells. The bell ringers use the bay under the tower and the counselling area was moved to the parish office.

There is a yard at street level at the west end of the church accessible through a passage from St Mary's Row. Into this yard the Army was persuaded to use one of its very big mobile cranes to lift a pressurised water vessel. This was connected to the church heating and a brick hut built around it. During off-peak times two industrial electric water heaters heat water to near boiling point, which is then pumped under pressure to the tank. It is then released when needed to heat the church. It is surprisingly cost effective and we know of no other system quite like it.

At this time, Rose Cottage at the rear of the yard caught fire. It had been used by one of the businesses facing onto St Mary's Row to store records, most of which were lost either through burning or water damage. Funds were available from a bequest to repair Rose Cottage and to build a connecting block between it and the church. A new doorway through the west end of the church provided first floor access to the extended Rose Cottage. The Piggott Room was created for meetings and Sunday school teaching at first floor level, and the director of music, Mick Perrier, opened a sheet music retail business on the ground floor called Cottage Music, which continued for a number of years It is now used as extended Sunday school teaching space and for other meetings.

In the late 1990's, when Hayward Osborne was Vicar, the layout of the worship space was enhanced by building a raised dais for a nave altar in space previously occupied by pews. This allows the focus of worship to be brought forward into the body of the church instead of being almost out of earshot at the far end of the chancel.

The future of the church building is now in debate again, prompted by the loss of the Centre 13 facilities, and the desire to ensure the effective use of the large space within the church, currently occupied only for Sunday worship, mid-week services and other occasional activities. This large, prominent church building proudly occupying its 600 year old site, is a central feature of Moseley Village. Its 'raison d'etre' is as a place of worship. But its facilities, either within or added to it, should be available for use by the wider community. How this will be achieved is perhaps the story of the next 30 years.

Nigel Blakey

THE CHRISTIAN CHURCH

The church scene prior to the 1970s had changed little over the decades, the main churches being St. Anne's, St. Agnes' and St Mary's (all C of E), St Columba (United Reformed Church after the joining of the Congregational and Presbyterian Churches, and therefore with a strong Scottish connection), the Baptist Church and smaller ones such as Hope Chapel (Brethren). Up until this time, Cambridge Road Methodists and the Roman Catholics based in Church Road also considered themselves part of the Moseley Churches.

Then, in the 1970s, the traditional pattern began to change.

First, a phenomenon swept across the UK Church scene causing churches to emphasise their similarities rather than their differences, reflected in musicals such as *Come Together*, and *If My People*. By the early 1980s, Moseley Alive was bringing many Christians together of all persuasions in recognition of their relationship together. This grassroots coming together proved to be far more effective in uniting churches. Secondly, there was a greater awareness of the reality of the Holy Spirit as the charismatic movement had begun to affect both individuals and the life of the Churches.

These two factors led to the formation and growth of Riverside Church. Initially, in 1984, a group of Christians with a more relaxed and joyful style of worship sought to be a distinct congregation at St Mary's. However, after much discussion and agreement with all of the other leaders of Moseley and Kings Heath Churches, Riverside Church became the newest addition to the Moseley Church Scene. Meeting first in a house, then in Swanshurst School, it finally moved to Queensbridge School in 1990 and is now one of the largest in South Birmingham with an estimated congregation of 7-800 (many also from Kings Heath). It involves itself in the life of the school supporting it in as many ways as possible, such as in their Ofsted inspection in 2004 and in the equipping of its main hall. Riverside has a wide range of activities, from parenting courses to cleaning up a street and its front gardens.

Further changes occurred: in 1991, Moseley Baptist Church closed down due to the building being declared dangerous. It amalgamated with and moved to Kings Heath Baptist Church, forming the Moseley and Kings Heath Baptist Church. However, a new church had been meeting back in their hall and they finally obtained permission to buy the Baptist church and hall.

This became The Calvary Church of God in Christ, the second new church in Moseley. At first, they were unable to use the church building itself due to its dangerous state but, with the aid of gifts and heritage lottery money, were able to repair the whole building. It is wonderful to see this impressive Church building filled with praise and worship again.

The Calvary Church has added another dimension and flavour to Moseley Churches. Every year a service reflecting our Churches' unity is run in January: this is held at each church in rotation providing an amazing opportunity to experience a wide variety of worship styles from traditional Anglican, contemporary Anglican, URC, and black Pentecostal to charismatic Independent Church.

During the 1980s and 90s, the Churches also came together for Good Friday: first, in a procession with a large cross around the centre of Moseley or to one of the churches to hold a Service of Reflection. Secondly, August Sunday Evening Services were shared around the churches. Common ways of celebrating Easter still take place; St Mary's process with the cross to the Village Green in order to erect it there for Easter Week and hold a prayer vigil to greet the dawn on Easter Day, celebrating the resurrection of Christ. Joint Lent House Groups come and go. There is an increasing desire to build worthwhile relationships between the Churches and to seek other ways of expressing our oneness apart from the Christmas and Easter cards which contain all services: for example, a summer tennis afternoon, taking over Moseley Tennis Club in Billesley Lane.

At the same time that these two churches started, several other changes occurred to this pattern.

Firstly, Cambridge Road Methodist Church turned its focus to King's Heath. Although it has a B13 postcode, its location and congregation were predominantly towards the King's Heath High Street area. It has since become more of a part of that area rather than Moseley.

Secondly, St John's and St. Martin's Roman Catholic Church in Balsall Heath which was responsible for the development of a church based on their Community Hall in Church Road and RC School St Martin de Porres in Oakland Rd, decided to merge congregations into their existing Church in Balsall Heath. The Roman Catholics in Moseley thus worship either at St Dunstan's in King's Heath or St John's and St. Martin's.

Thirdly, St Anne's in Park Hill decided to turn their focus to Balsall Heath and to put their energies into that area. This caused a paradox with the Church being part of Moseley but not part of the Moseley Churches. It is only in 2004, with the decision to join together once more the parishes of St Anne and St Mary in what will become a United Benefice, that the original focus was restored and St Anne's effectively became part of Moseley again.

Fourthly, St Agnes has gradually evolved in its ethos and worship styles. In the 1970s, it was a traditional middle-of-the-road Anglican church, and then, in the 80s and 90s, became more informal in its worship style. At the present time St Agnes is enjoying a breadth of styles of worship, valuing both traditional and informal (in different contexts) and has been rediscovering the importance of the Bible in the Christian life. St Agnes aims to be a friendly church where everyone is welcome. Together with Riverside Church, St Agnes' recognises the importance of small groups - where people can be cared for, where they can get to know each other really well, and where friends and neighbours can be invited to share in meals and friendship. Both churches have also developed ALPHA courses where people both within and outside the church can question and discuss faith and spiritual issues in a non-threatening environment.

Fifthly, while the Scottish roots of St Columba United Reformed Church have long influenced its church life, the church has welcomed a large contingent of members of Ghanaian origin which has greatly enriched the church fellowship.

Lastly, the latest addition to the Churches is the Congregational Church of Brazil. Services are in a mixture of Portuguese and English and are held for the moment (in 2004) in the Moseley CDT in the Post Office Building.

The Moseley Churches thus reflect the amazing spectrum of people living in Moseley. They hold the paradox of continually adapting and changing yet providing stability and the sense of the majesty and awesomeness of God that never changes. We must never be surprised at this, but be encouraged to dip our feet into this River of God, that we call the Moseley Churches.

David Isgrove,
Chair of the Moseley Churches 2004

RELIGIOUS DIVERSITY

Muslim

According to the Sunday Mercury (December 15th, 1946) there were about a thousand Muslims living in the whole of Birmingham at that time; Arab Muslims worshipped at their Mosque in Edward Road; Indian at theirs in Speedwell Road.

In the last sixty years, there has been a great expansion of the Muslim population and hence, the mosques that serve them.

Early in 2003, the Muslim community, who have a centre, the Jamia Mosque Hanza Islamic Centre at the junction of Church Road and St. Alban's Road, decided to begin outreach to other religious communities. They chose to meet at a neutral space and have organised several meetings for dialogue in the Moseley Community Development Trust building. The meetings included representatives from the Church of England, Methodist, URC and Roman Catholic communities. At the Moseley Festival 2004, this group organised a stall to give information and advice on faith matters. This community consists of families coming from the same area of north Pakistan and are known as Chach Pathans. Most Chachi's speak Hindko, pronounced 'Hinko', which has a close resemblance to Punjabi and Urdu. They are the most central group to Moseley.

When the Roman Catholic Mass Centre at St. Albans Road was sold in 1977, leaving behind the Voluntary Aided parish primary school of St. Martin de Porres in Forest Road, the St. Alban's Road Centre relocated their place of worship in Woodstock Road. Currently, the Chachis are constructing a full-scale mosque in Willows Road, and Willows Crescent as well as numerous Muslim prayer rooms which will cater for Muslims of differing sectarian or national identities, for example, the Deobandi and Barelwi, or Alawiites.

Buddhist

In the Moseley area, there is a centre of the Western Buddhist Order and (separately) the International headquarters of the Western Buddhist Order.

The Buddhist community has a particularly strong presence in Moseley, since the Western Buddhist Order has a monastic Headquarters at 'Mamyaloka', 30 Chantry Road, and an Associate Centre with a major shrine room in Park Road. The Buddhist Headquarters in Chantry Road is the home of the founder of the Western Buddhist Order, Ven. Sangharakshita, who is now in retirement. The Park Road Centre, which include a bookshop, occupies what was once a Jewish synagogue belonging to the Orthodox community. On selling the synagogue, the Jewish community continued to hold synagogue in the King David Primary School.

Jewish

The Jewish community is centred on King David's primary school, where synagogue continues to be held. King David's is a Voluntary Aided faith school with Jewish ethos and curriculum, though pupils are taken from all faiths. The Lubavitch Jewish Education Trust has a youth service centre with its own Rabbi in Willows Road; this centre concentrates on charitable work.

Sikh

There are, in the area, three Gurudwaras (dedicated to gurus such as Guru Gobind Singh or Guru Nanak)

It is heartening perhaps to reiterate that many Sikhs and Moslems send their children to local schools such as King David's (Jewish) and St. John and St. Monica's and St. Martin de Porres (both Roman Catholic). It is amongst the young in Moseley schools, and in the regular interfaith meetings at the Community Trust building, that religious understanding and tolerance may continue to develop.

Bill Ozanne

PART THREE : INSTITUTIONS

THE MOSELEY BOG

Moseley Bog owes its existence to its relationship with Sarehole Mill, its survival to the Save Our Bog Campaign, led by Joy Fifer and its fame to JRR Tolkien.

Just three miles south of the city is a green oasis, a Local Nature Reserve extending over nearly 28 acres. There are three distinct landscapes: the Victorian Gardens to the north, wild wet, boggy woodland in the centre and new woodland, Joy's Wood, with meadows to the south. You can escape to find solitude and peace and a sense of magic and mystery. There's Bluebell Wood, a babbling brook, numerous springs and boggy hollows, fallen trees and a secret pool. There is a rich diversity of plant life, 55 recorded species of birds and over one hundred species of fungi. Squirrels abound and if you are lucky you will see rabbits.

The Doomsday Book indicates an area of meadow, bog and pasture and woodland. In 1629, the land, which was part of the ancient manor of Yardley, became associated with Moseley when it was acquired by the Grevis family who lived at Moseley Hall.

Moseley Bog, now a unique urban wetland, was once Moseley Old or Great Pool. Around 1750, an earth dam was built to create a reserve pool to supplement the small millpond at Sarehole and power the water mill which had been in existence since at least 1542. Great Pool, which appears on a rental roll of 1781, was fed by the Coldbath Brook which starts in Kings Heath and flows for two miles across the estate of Greethurst (Moseley Golf Course since 1892) and the common land of Wake Green and Swanshurst Common until it joins the River Cole near Sarehole Mill. It fed 4 pools, all fish ponds harvested by nets.

There are many botanical references to rare plants recorded as growing in Moseley Wake Green and bogs and pools on Moseley Common before the enclosure of Moseley Wake Green around 1840, and the subsequent drainage of the boggy land. Dr.William Ick, Secretary of the Philosophic Society of Birmingham, published lists of rarities in 'The Analyst' in 1837 including the Wood Horsetail in 'Moseley Bog' and the Royal Fern on 'Moseley Common.' Noted botanist Miss MA Beilby confirmed his sightings in the same year. By 1867, 'The Botany of Worcestershire' describes the botanical interest of 'the pools and relics of bogs ......chiefly retrospective.'

During the nineteenth century, Sarehole Mill reverted from metal working back to corn milling and, together with the installation of a steam engine in 1853, reduced its requirement for waterpower. It is thought that Old Pool Meadow below the Great Pool was waterlogged, possibly because the dam was leaking. By 1858, the dam had been breached, the brick sluice broken down and the pool was drained. At some subsequent time drainage ditches were dug across the bed of the former pool, but the land with its numerous springs never completely drained and was never reclaimed. Nature took its course and created wild wet woodland, a genuine new bog complete with sphagnum moss.

During the later Victorian period houses were built along Wake Green Road with gardens extending to the edge of the developing bog. The remains of the Old Gardens, greenhouse foundations and landscaping are visible today and at their best when the rhododendrons are in bloom.

In 1896, the young JRR Tolkien moved into 264 Wake Green Road with his widowed mother and little brother Hilary. They stayed and played for four years. Seventy years later he recalled in an interview with The Guardian 'a kind of lost paradise. There was an old mill that really did grind corn, with two millers, a great big pond with swans on it, a sandpit, a wonderful dell with flowers, a few old fashioned village houses, and, further away, a stream with another mill... I could draw you a map of every inch of it. I loved it with an intense love.' But in the foreword to The Lord of the Rings in 1954 he laments ' the country in which I lived in childhood was being shabbily destroyed before I was ten.'

The process of suburban encirclement of the Bog continued during the twentieth century with farms and fields giving way to housing developments along Wake Green Road, Swanshurst Lane, and Yardley Wood Road. There were postwar prefabs, which were removed in 1977, council housing in Thirlmere Drive in the sixties and sporadic infill elsewhere.

In 1935, Birmingham City Council Education Department bought Moseley Bog and an adjacent valley to the south, then known as The Dell. The Dell was an area of fields, meadows and osier beds through which flowed the Coldbath Brook. Sadly, the City used it as a tip during the post war rebuilding of Birmingham and in the 1970s the tip was capped and the valley filled in to create playing fields. The Coldbath Brook disappeared underground to re-emerge in the Bog. Ironically the playing fields were never popular because of poor drainage.

In 1976, Mr Godrey Nall, a keen amateur naturalist read an old article in *The Bromsgrove Messenger* by naturalist Fred Fincher who wrote about the possiblity that part of the old Moseley Bog that had fascinated Victorian botanists might still exist. Godfrey checked out the map, caught the bus and clambered down the slope beyond St Bernard's School playground in Wake Green Road. He found himself in "a magical place with an atmosphere of seclusion and forgotteness" and with impressive plants and wildlife. He wrote to the City Planning Department urging its preservation as a wildlife area. The City forwarded his letter to the Nature Conservancy Council and in 1977 the NCC Regional Officer, George Barker, asked Godfrey to show him the site. George Barker was impressed with the bog, stream and pool, the wet and dry woodland, the birds and the plantlife and particularly, a rare Wood Horsetail, Equisetum Sylvestris. His report recommended that the site be designated a Site of Special Scientific Interest and commended its potential as an educational nature reserve.

Godfrey sent the NCC Report to the Education Department who began to appreciate that they had more than a few soggy playing fields on their books. They responded with proposals to set up a management scheme for the site and to use it as an educational resource. In 1978, Godfrey was invited to join a Bog Management Committee, chaired by Bill Graham of King Edward's School, Aston, who were looking for a conservation management project. Under the guidance of the Management Committee, which also had representation from the NCC and the Education Department, the pupils from KES researched and surveyed the Bog area and undertook a range of practical management work.

One day, in 1980, the school party bumped into some surveyors tramping through the Old Victorian Gardens and soon established that the Diocesan Schools Commission, who owned the land, were submitting a Planning Application for 22 detached houses in what is now Pool Meadow Close. The Management Committee and the NCC objected to the application, concerned about the dire impact that such a development would have upon the delicate ecology of the bog. There was, for example, a line of springs running across the bottom of the Old Gardens crucially helping to maintain the water table in the Bog. They also leafleted the local residents including that "stalwart, dynamic, enthusiastic, unrelenting campaigner", *Joy Fifer.*

Joy Fifer

Joy and Alan Fifer, nature lovers both, lived right opposite on Wake Green Road.

They walked their dog in Moseley Bog and their four children had played in the woods over the road. "We've got to do something" was Joy's response. She rang Friends of the Earth for initial advice, delivered some new leaflets, called a public meeting and wondered if anyone would turn up. 300 people packed the hall. "I'd never attended a public meeting before, let alone chaired one, I was so scared I was actually shaking." The six year struggle of the 'Save Our Bog' campaign took off "morning, noon and night" recalls Joy's daughter Gaby. Joy rallied all the local residents and environmentalists from near and far. Within a few weeks, a 12,500-signature petition was presented, 500 letters of objection were delivered to the Planning Department, and Joy and some other residents joined the Bog Management Committee. Local councillors got their boots muddy as they were taken to see the Bog, wildlife celebrities like Bill Oddie and Richard Maybe were recruited and there was intense local and national media coverage.

In 1982, the planning application for the Old Gardens and another from NEC Homes for an adjacent development of nine properties were rejected. The applicants were advised that favourable consideration would be given to amended schemes incorporating a a buffer zone to be conveyed to the City between reduced developments and the Bog. In 1986, the City acquired the vital portion of the Old Gardens containing the spring line as part of the Moseley Bog site and planning permission was granted for only 11 houses instead of 22.

In 1986, the triumphant Save Our Bog campaign became the Moseley Bog Conservation Group and in 1987 was involved in the planting of native trees and shrubs on the old Dell playing fields.

In 1989, management of the site was taken over by the Millstream Rangers and in 1991 Moseley Bog and The Dell were declared a Local Nature Reserve. In 1997, 300 volunteer hours were contributed to the Heritage Ponds Project co-ordinated by the World Wide Fund for Nature. A sleeper walkway was constructed to minimise erosion of the dam and silt was removed from the pond.

In 1982, a 3000-year-old Bronze Age burnt mound was identified along the Colebath Brook in Moseley Bog. In 1998, Joy launched an appeal to construct a boardwalk to protect the burnt mound. The public response to sponsoring a railway sleepers at £15 each was excellent. With additional thanks to Railtrack, there is now a protective boardwalk that has also considerably improved public access to the Bog. In 2002, following an assessment by English Heritage, the burnt mounds were designated Scheduled Ancient Monuments.

The new woodland area and the meadow and hedgerow formerly known as The Dell was renamed Joy's Wood in 1999 in recognition of Joy Fifer's contribution and in 2001 Joy was awarded the MBE for services to nature conservation.

It is proposed that the Leisure and Culture Department should take over the landholding from Education in conjunction with the Wildlife Trust for Birmingham and the Black Country taking over the lease of the site. Heads of Terms are agreed and hoped to go ahead in 2004. The Wildlife Trust is applying for Heritage Lottery Funding to secure the controlled development and preservation of Moseley Bog, which I am so lucky to have at the bottom of my garden.

Stephanie Silk

INSTITUTIONS

MOSELEY PARK AND POOL

Moseley Park has been offering keys for rent since 1899. The origins are well known but may bear repetition; the Park, with its Pool and Icehouse, were designed by Humphry Repton and were part of the grounds of Moseley Hall until Salisbury Road cut the estate in half in 1896. Building land was as acutely short in Moseley then as it apparently is now, and there was a gloomy assumption that this beautiful area to the North of Salisbury Road would soon be filled with Edwardian villas. However, some local businessmen stepped in and bought it to keep as a Park, initially perhaps for their own pleasure. Very soon, they were offering - through an agent - a key to anyone in Moseley whose family were prepared to pay £1 a year.

There was a predisposition at that time to keep this arrangement for the locals, and there are to this day people from Edgbaston or Kings Heath who ask if they are 'allowed' to join. The answer, now and in the future, is 'yes!'

In the last thirty years, according to ex-Moseley people who come back to have another look, the Park itself has changed very little in its appearance - trees have matured, some have come down; Canada Geese have arrived to general irritation; the Pool has silted up a little more; the Icehouse has been wonderfully restored by the Moseley Society. But there have been dramatic changes of a different sort.

The Park is no longer a slightly exclusive domain for three or four hundred families as it was, say, in 1980; the term 'private park' is out of date. It has eleven hundred key-holding families, and rising. Public events are no longer regarded as unwelcome invasions - the Moseley Festival has been in the Park on and off for seven years now, there is a festival of gypsy jazz music, there are many open days, so that anyone can look round the Icehouse, there is Shakespeare, an under-16 open angling contest round the Pool - and so on. There are three part-time rangers as well as the Park Manager to keep things in good order. Each year, there is a public meeting of keyholders to discuss plans for the future.

There is much more to be done of this sort - the Park management hope to raise the finance to build a visitor centre in a couple of years, the beautiful Dell area by the boathouse has been cleared of rubbish, and there is an agreement with DEFRA (which used to be the Ministry of Agriculture) to work together in carrying out long term restoration of the Park because of its historic importance.

Local people for miles around - not just Moseley people - now regard the Park as their own secret garden, especially perhaps those in flats or otherwise without access to open space of their own. The phenomenon continues to be that, despite the great increase in membership, the Park usually appears to be empty.

The tiny non-profit-making company, Moseley Park and Pool Co Ltd, continues to run this priceless Moseley facility, quietly, without pay and without fuss. It is now one of the oldest surviving companies in Birmingham. Long may it continue. A key to the Park may be obtained from their agents Chamberlains Estate Agents, 27 St Mary's Row, Moseley. Tel no. 0121 442 4040.

John Williams

INSTITUTIONS

BIRMINGHAM 13

Birmingham 13 is a monthly magazine, named after the postal district where we live. It has now been appearing for 31 years and is therefore an interesting source as to what was perceived by successive editors to be of interest to Moseley people during that time. For many years, it was called *birmingham 13* (with a small b) to distinguish it (for some reason) from the postal district. It should be emphasized perhaps that it described itself as a church magazine for much of the period under review. The chair has always been a Christian minister; the strength of the religious affiliation has however been variable, reflecting perhaps the interests of successive editors.

The first issue in 1973 couldn't have been more tentative - 4 pages of mainly church news, accompanied by something called 'Compass' - supplied perhaps from the diocesan office – to bulk it up. This arrangement continued until March 1975, when 'Compass' shut down and *'birmingham 13'* took a deep breath and felt strong enough to go it alone.

The first editor was Michael Shoesmith who worked at the BBC; the chairman was Stephen Beck, vicar at St Agnes' Church and the original idea seems to have come from Michael Blood who was then the curate. Stephen was a stalwart friend of the paper: "Why a community newspaper, why a community newspaper by churches?" he asked. "Not because everything we say will be about churches, or true because we say it is. It is because we have an interest, a prejudice if you like. We believe it is a good thing for people to understand each other, to care for each other and to help each other. . . if we have ignored part of the area in which you live, the answer is in your hands."

As to content, the stage was set straight away for a battle which was to continue for the next 15 years, between Moseley people and an obdurate West Midlands County Council. The very first issue published a startling map showing a great 4-lane highway, planned for 1975-6, coming through Kings Heath and running more or less along the railway line through Moseley but still taking down some 250 houses in its path.

Trafalgar Road was particularly at risk, and planning blight (not being able to sell your house because of half-revealed plans for its possible destruction) a real worry. The heart of the problem was the perceived impact of the M40 - not yet complete - and the expected stream of heavy lorries which would pour through South Birmingham. There was a crucial difference between GIA's (General Improvement Areas) and RA's (Renewal Areas). If you chanced to be in the former, it meant that you might get a free new roof and other benefits; the latter was not so good, since it involved bulldozers.

It is difficult to think oneself back into such a time, when zonal planning brooked no argument. Early editions of *'Birmingham 13'* report the plans but make no comment; there is no hint that anyone might argue with the Council as to whether the plans were good ones. However, such imperious behaviour at the Council House may have

John Haslam
A past Chairman of Birmingham 13

James Hutchison
An outstanding photographer recording Moseley life

 *Thirteen*

belonged to the 'sixties rather than the 'seventies; a new scepticism was in the air. Early in 1974, a letter - in my view, a historic letter - was published from one Paul Brown of Cambridge Road, pointing out that the so-called bye-pass went smack through Moseley, cutting the community in two. "Why was *Birmingham 13'* not objecting, rather than lamely reporting?" he asked. There must have been anxious words at the next editorial meeting. Anyway, his letter worked, and a generation of stroppy Moseleyites was born. 'Big business stands to gain or lose a great deal when these plans are finalised' thundered an editorial the following month. They'd caught on.

Centre 13 (a name which was thought up later) was opened on the site of the old Church of England School to enormous excitement and with Jackanory, Alcoholics Anonymous, over 60's, cubs, scouts, weightlifting lessons (four times a week!), acrobatics, whist, drama, upholstery, flower arranging, dressmaking, keep fit, barn dances, fashion shows and wedding receptions. A free library was launched there in 1974, which soon had 4000 books and fifty members, but Tesco had opened that year (where Quiksave is now) and then bought three adjacent shops in July, to general concern as to the future of the shopping centre; Mr. Lunt was chairman of Moseley Park and remarked that anyone could become a member provided they did not bring a firearm into the Park; MDCC, one of the many drama groups (and happily still performing each year in Moseley Park), was putting on a play called 'The 1861 Whitby Lifeboat Disaster' at St Columba's Church Hall.

When North Sea gas came in, we all had to have some new gadget fitted to our gas supply. It was reported that during an all day vigil at St Columba's Church, visitors were asked to sign a visitors' book and give their reason for attending. Halfway down, an entry read 'The gas man - to see about your conversion.'

In May 1974, Geoffrey Mobsby made the first known suggestion that central Moseley might be a Conservation Area (though as early as November 1968 Chantry Road and Park Hill Residents' Association had been putting together a 'comprehensive development plan to be drawn up for the area and submitted to the Council for their approval'). In June, the first Moseley Festival (called the Arts Festival) was held. It made a loss - no great surprize there, but, as ever, it seems to have pleased the readers. Also that June was published an ill-tempered sort of letter (signed 'a Moseley GP') about another theme which was to raise local temperatures, one way or another, for the next thirty-odd years; Moseley was being taken over by probationers, ex-prisoners, battered wives, drug addicts, prostitutes; the 'filth' was ankle deep; we were over-extending ourselves in social 'care in the community' (interesting phrase for 1974) - it was time for the clergy to ring the church bells in alarm; Moseley was in danger!

The following month (July 1974) there was a response from Heather Harrison; Moseley (she explained) was different from other suburbs. We have contrasting classes and groups; physical, mental and emotional problems were not confined to foreigners or the poor. We had no right to sweep things not easy of solution under someone else's carpet. "Why Moseley?" the GP had asked. "Why not?" replied Heather. "Moseley would become a unique community . . it will afford places for those who cannot fit very easily into modern life. Moseley is not sterile, but shows compassion in action . . . and will not only survive but survive with a healthy heart." Needless to say, Heather Harrison was editor of the paper not so long after.

Thus, in the first year or so of publication, the first editor was unwittingly setting out the themes for many future issues - threats from planning, concern about society's dropouts, conservation, supermarkets and their impact on shops, the sometimes uncertain finances of the Moseley Festival - and, not least, the enormous energies for good in this community unleashed through the opening of Centre 13.

So the subject matter for many of the 350-odd front pages had been suggested; yet from the late 'seventies on, it is the peculiar, the out-of-the-way, that catches the eye. In May '75, there was an appeal for black and white TV sets 'lying idle in many homes after the pre-budget rush to buy colour sets'. Who for? For single old people, for whom they could offer 'many hours of enjoyment'. In the same month, the total income of Moseley car park was reliably estimated at £15 a week.

That Autumn, there was a great influx of antique shops - five in all; the paper was impatient, treating them rather as a later editor treated the influx of pubs. Plannning applications were now available for everyone to look at for the first time. It was noted that there were three bakers (Lukers was already 107 years old), four butchers, three general stores, three grocers, and two supermarkets, though I cannot think where the other supermarket was then thought to be. And even with this splendid choice, there was anxiety about a decline in shopping - "those who shop in Kings Heath have lost the right to complain!" Also that Autumn, Elizabeth Way became Birmingham secretary of the United Nations, and I am delighted to point out that she still is.

By Christmas, the fish and chip club had had to close down because of the high price of potatoes; on the other hand, Beryl Chempin, the international piano teacher in Moorcroft Road, was living and eating in her kitchen because her house had broken in two because of subsidence. Moseley Rugby Club was attacked for its high entry price of £1 (a ticket to an England/Wales international apparently cost 80p).

And in another gas-man story, in the Spring of '87, David Cummings in Oxford Road was the hero, having proved that his gas meter was 'jumping' despite fierce opposition from the Gas Board. It was noticed that the £149 reluctantly returned to him was in the form of a credit note against future use, rather than in the form of a cheque.

That Summer, there was much distress in the Roman Catholic community when St Martin de Porres merged, almost overnight, with St John's, Balsall Heath. A plan to build a new church on the corner of Church Road and St Albans Road was abandoned. The first signs of trouble for Sorrento Maternity Hospital also emerged - there was talk of feasability appraisals and rationalization. The following year, the local man from the Area Health Authority was to call Sorrento 'an obstetric slum', but most people who had had direct contact with Sorrento loved it to bits.

In the '70s and '80s, the paper was always around to welcome new ventures into the area. When one antique dealer was asked "Why Moseley?" he replied, "Well, it's Birmingham's Chelsea." There was a trend, people trying to place Moseley by comparing us to somewhere else - a hopeless task. Another described us as "equivalent to Greenwich Village in New York"; and when Timaeus Art Gallery opened at the top of Salisbury Road, Moseley was described as as 'an area most receptive to the arts - like Hampstead perhaps'.

The paper continued to enjoy its April Fools, whether the readers appreciated them or not. There had been the very first one, way back, about the lavatories on the Green being bought by an American and taken to Texas; or the same lavatories being converted into a tube station to take members of the CBSO to perform at the Town Hall. Others had Moseley as an independent republic, à la *Passport to Pimlico*, with a five-year tax rebate, our own passports, and a six-nations rugby cup to include Moseley. Or there was the all too believable one about a huge lap dancing club on the Reddings site, parking for 250 cars, and special club membership for Moor Green Lane Residents. . .

It's not quite the same without a good story on the front cover, though the photographs continue to be very good. Our favourite front cover ever, which was stuck up in many a shop window by sympathetic tradesmen, was 'Never Mind Maastricht - what about an economic policy for Moseley!'

Still, from 'Cougar Annie's Garden in Canada' to 'Mother Bunnie goes shopping', we've covered pretty well everything over the years. But never forget what our founders said - 'if we have ignored your area of Moseley, the answer is in your hands - tell us your story!'

John Williams

INSTITUTIONS

LOCAL SCIENTISTS

Moseley's proximity to Birmingham's two main Universities, as well as being quite handy for Warwick, has long been a lure for the various academics looking for somewhere to live which was not as crowded as Harborne or did not have the feeling of lacking a centre like Edgbaston. Among those who made their homes in Moseley were many distinguished scientists, who found that the ambience in the village gave them, perhaps, a feeling of the country more than a large city; and for some Edgbaston Cricket Club may have been an attraction withing walking distance.

Birmingham has had links with leading scientists over many years. The University made a very important contribution, in the person of Rudolph Peierls, to the Manhattan Project, the American atom bomb programme which, had it been lost to the Germans, the world would have been a very different place today. And they were not too far behind. Also the cavity magnetron, which was vital to the development of radar, was designed and built in Birmingham University. Some internationally famed figures in their field are living in Moseley, a selection of whom are profiled below.

Professor J. D. Dowell FRS

John Dowell's field is particle physics; trying to understand what everything is made of and how it is all put together. Apart from the time spent at CERN, the European particle accelerator, in 1960-62 and again in 1973-74, and some time spent in America 1968-69, he has been at Birmingham University. The main instrument of the particle physicist is the particle accelerator. It takes protons, for instance, and shoots them at very high speeds, close to the speed of light, and crashes them against materials, or into other protons travelling in the other direction, and measures the resultant patterns. Magnets surround the point of contact and cause different types of particles, with different energies and charges, to take different paths. There can be up to 1000 million collisions per second. With immense patience and expertise, the paths are analysed and the nature of the particles defined. Although more than 200 different particles have been discovered, it is believed that there are only two basic ones; leptons, which include electrons, and quarks. He is extremely proud that he now holds the chair of the Poynting Professor of Physics, which Sir Mark Oliphant once held. Mark Oliphant, an Australian, came to Birmingham in the 1930s and built Europe's first particle accelerators, the Cyclotron and the Synchrotron. John's team now co-operate closely with other universities, in particular Hamburg, and Stanford in California, the cost of experiments on the accelerators now being prohibitive for a single university. He has been a Fellow of the Royal Society, perhaps the most prestigious science organisation in the world, since 1986, and in 1988 was awarded the Rutherford Medal and Prize of the Institute of Physics.

Professor Maj Hulten

Maj is Swedish and early in her career, which has been complex and variable, had an experience which certainly must have catapulted her into the area of genetics. In southern Sweden there was work going on on mouse and plant cells. She went there and said she wanted to work on human cells. But mice were the best they could offer. She designed elaborate experiments, which meant sampling cells every four hours round the clock. During one of these samplings, on 23rd December 1955, she was tapped on the shoulder by a visiting Chinese scientist, Joe Hin Tjio. He said "Would you like to see something interesting? perhaps you could come to my room." Peering down the microscope she saw there, for the first time ever, human chromosomes. This event in fact showed that there were only 46 chromosomes in humans rather than the 48 which was then believed. Virtually every cell in the body has these chromosomes. We inherit 23 from each parent, and the DNA, which is contained in these determine our inborn characteristics. She realised immediately that chromosome investigation was going to be a very important tool to unravel reasons for physical deformities and learning disabilities in people. She came to Birmingham in 1975 and later moved to Warwick University, where she has been continuing her work in many areas of chromosome abnormalities. She is the medical advisor for some support groups of parents of children damaged by rare chromosome abnormalities. One of these is an organisation called Unique which was initiated by Maj, and she helped to finance a computer database which is accumulating knowledge of how these children will develop.

Professor Peter Willmore

Peter took his PhD in atomic physics at University College London, and had returned there as a research fellow when he was invited to become involved in the infant British Rocket programme in the late 1950's. Because of his involvement, he was given the opportunity to visit the States when the Americans generously invited other nations to participate in their space programme. It was here that Peter and some other British scientists were able to carry out some very important experiments. The Americans had captured the German V2 weapons, along with their creator Werner Von Braun, but because this was not politically correct just after the 1939-45 conflagration, they had to pretend that their main interest was scientific. This was of considerable advantage to the scientists, who had no wish to blow up half the world, and Peter and his friends were able to use the situation to their advantage. They were able to obtain the first recordings of the temperature of much of the earth and discovered to their amazement that the temperature at 400 kilometres over the North and South poles was actually a blistering 1000°C, thanks to the magnetic field around the earth which directed electrons to rise from the poles. Peter became Professor of Physics at Birmingham in 1972, and helped Birmingham to become one of the foremost Universities in the country in space research.

Professor Colin Gough

Colin is professor of high temperature superconductivity at Birmingham University. Superconductivity is the strange quality possessed by some materials which enables them to conduct electricity indefinitely without the need for a further input of energy. The high temperature that is mentioned is, in fact, 150° degrees below zero. If a material could be discovered that would superconduct at room temperature the world would be transformed and much cheaper means of providing electricity could be achieved. This is what physicists the world over are seeking, although the material may not ever exist. Superconductivity is already used to generate the large fields for MRI medical imaging machines in the QE and other large hospitals, enabling us to look inside the body without harmful radiation. It also levitates the world's fastest 'maglev' trains in Japan - 540 kmh. It was quite possible that Colin could have been lost to physics had he chosen instead to follow the other profession he was eminently qualified for - music. His family have been musicians for at least three generations, perhaps more. His great-grandfather was leader of the Royal Philharmonic Society. Colin was leader of the National Youth Orchestra, when he faced the agonising decision of whether to make music or physics his career. He had been a junior exhibitor at the Royal College of Music and was under considerable pressure to be a professional violinist. However, he opted for physics, to the benefit of Birmingham University.

Professor Alan Rickinson

The reason that Alan became a virologist and ended up chasing a virus called the Epstein-Barr virus is a story not that unusual. He was very influenced by a teacher, "Bug Allen", who taught him biology in his first two years at grammar school. "Bug Allen" had 'lived'. He had actually spent his student years on a barge on the Seine in Paris, and recounted to his fascinated class his life there and the bad language of the French bargees' wives. When Alan went to Cambridge in 1962, and was uncertain whether to take chemistry, biochemistry or physics, perhaps the memory of "Bug" gave to 'bio' a glamour it would not otherwise have possessed. So Alan took biochemistry and stayed to take a PhD. The building he worked in at the time was probably the most famous laboratory in the world in that area. Francis Crick of DNA fame was still there, and Alan was taught by Max Perutz, another Nobel laureate. The Epstein-Barr virus has links with a certain type of leukaemia in Africa, with Hodgkins disease in this country and with nasal cancer found largely in China. Another part of Alan's research is to find out what else is involved in the actual development of the cancer.

These are just a few of the many 'Moseley Scientists' who have made substantial contributions to the advance of knowledge through our fine local Universities. There are many others of whom we can also be very proud.

David Leeson

PART FIVE : LEISURE

THE MOSELEY FESTIVAL

Looking through old copies of *Birmingham 13* to try to establish a pattern for the Moseley Festival, one is struck by the cyclical nature of the event; a team is formed, enormous energy is expended, new events introduced, money is either made or lost. This would continue for three or four years, and then perhaps the team might fall apart - some would leave, others might join; but there might also be a perception on the part of the committee that they had noticed that 'nobody was helping them.' Events would fall away, we might be left with little more than the street fair; but then - nearly always - a new team would move in and a new cycle would start.

Something like this has continued to this day.

The first Moseley Festival that I can find on record was that in June 1975 - so, like St Mary's Church, the festival organisers will also be celebrating in 2005 - their 30th anniversary.

This first one was described as a 'Community Arts Festival' and, like many which followed, was highly ambitious; a children's sports day, a sponsored walk, an Old-time Music-Hall, a Jazz Night, a performance of *'Macbeth'* and a Festival Barbecue - not a bad start.

Centre 13 was the headquarters for 1976 - it was described as a hive of activity - 'workshops every night, last minute arrangements, intense excitement in the days leading up to the Festival' (the Community Arts title had already been dropped). It went on for two weeks, again in June. The All Services Club was to be a performance area - as was St Mary's Church. Individual streets were encouraged to organise their own events; the main committee was seen as a 'planning and coordination' body. Certainly, I counted some sixty events in the programme, which is impressive. One of them was a public debate on 'the role of the Festival and the nature of community life in Moseley' between Ivor Bartlett (who ran the Fighting Cocks), John Luker (the baker), Albert Bore (you've heard of him), and the Rev David Good from St Agnes Church.

1977 was no less ambitious, introducing a tug-of-war on the village green, a village idiot contest, the Guiliani String Quartet at the Fighting Cocks and a 'six hour rock concert headed by Ricky Cool and the Icebergs' in Cannon Hill Park. 1978's Festival broadsheet has not survived; there was certainly a Festival but there is an absence of comment in *'Birmingham 13'* The headquarters were now at St Columba's Hall; can anyone remember?

1979, again a two-week affair, brought in the Beatles and Stones Disco, one of the most durable gigs, always subsequently described as 'Moseley's sweatiest event'. Fiddlers Three (Messrs Ballard, Sanders and McFadyen) were playing at St Agnes' Church, and the Birmingham Eisler Band and the Clarion Singers were playing music from 'the last years of the Weimar Republic'. Moseley Mastermind, a tough quiz, collectively answered by teams of four, made its first appearance; UB 40, in their early days, were playing in the Arena at MAC. But I do recall that there was an overall loss that year, and there was a need for a new-look committee in 1980 - which is exactly what came about.

So in 1980 Dave Cox became the chairman, Bill Hulse was to run publicity, Marjorie Hepburn Secretary, Mary Wells the Street Parade. The Festival was compressed into three days only. The intention was to give it a wider appeal - more of a street-fair for families and children, with lights and bunting, fewer minority interests.

In 1981, UB 40 were back at the Arena, and at no charge. The central event would be the street procession, getting everyone involved. Dave Cox's second year again stuck to three days, but there was to be a hot-air balloon in Moseley Park and the first of the nine-mile Moseley Marathons, which were to be so popular. The street fair had grown rapidly; this and the Parade had now become central events. Later, there was a long list of donations to local charities.

The following year, there were 1500 runners in the Moseley Marathon, a wonderful oldtime Music-hall in the Fighting Cocks and a gruelling two-day Moseley Mastermind. The Villagers put on their own extraordinary version of the Bible story of *'Jacob'*, written by Tony Shobrook. But it rained heavily, the pig-roast in Moseley Park had to be cancelled, and Dave Cox had £150 of his bunting and two of his loudspeakers stolen; this cast a distinct shadow, and we began to wonder how long Dave could continue to pour his energies - and finance - into the Festival.

1983, however, seemed as ambitious as ever - looking back, it is noticeable that the concentration into three days had been abandoned and things seemed to be going on for up to two weeks - perhaps a mistake. However, the focus was still on the street fair and the Moseley Marathon, which had become nice little earners (the stallholders paid for their stalls, the Marathon runners for running!) There was also a Festival Ball at the County Ground, which may - again with hindsight - have been somewhat over the top. But there were three bands in the Procession, which had some highly inventive floats. St Martin de Porres School I recall as always good for a surprize on Procession Day.

1984 was Dave Cox's last Festival - the vogue for marathons was passing, and 'only 550' ran that year. But there is no doubt that older Moseley people tend to measure the Festivals of today against the Dave Cox years, which were an exciting time. New Festival organisers could doubtless do without such hoary comparisons, but times have changed.

The 1985 Festival had a new committee headed by Bob Hartrick, the insurance broker who was sadly killed in a car accident a few years later. There was still a 'half-marathon' and Moseley Mastermind flourished; but the Festival was cut back to a week and the weather was wet throughout.

In 1986, the weather was much better, 650 ran the Marathon and the stalls along the Parade continued to grow in number and variety, apparently stretching the full length of the shopping centre on both sides of the road - which is always the sign of a good Festival with plenty of community participation.

In 1987, older readers will recall that we had an arcade, roughly where O'Neils pub is now. This was converted into a roofed theatre with a hundred seats. Organiser Steve Maddocks said that the drama groups sold out for every performance - does anyone remember what plays were put on? Mastermind drew 22 teams of four. Rosemary Burkhill captained the winning team. Tickets for the Beatles and Stones Disco at the Fighting Cocks were 'like gold dust' that year. One Claire Lindley won the 12-16 art prize.

The years from 1988 to 1992 were undoubtedly the Festival's darkest years. This may have reflected a general gloom in Moseley itself - it is hard to tell now. But the general tone of *Birmingham 13* reflects a declining shopping centre; *Birmingham 13* was itself going through a bad time, having come close to closure, so coverage of any events was limited.

However, in 1992, it ran a front page with the heading 'What, no Moseley Festival?' There was a public meeting in September with John Haslam in the chair. A new committee was formed for 1993, and another great surge of successful Moseley Festivals began.

'The patient nearly died, and is still in a delicate state,' said the headline. It was to be entirely a street fair plus a procession - yet it still raised £2000 for charities. Which raises a point in itself, much discussed at Festival committees over the years: is the Festival mainly to give people a good time, or is it mainly to raise money for charity? The 'good time' option has been much more favoured in recent years, mainly because of one sad fact: many of the charities for which money was raised in the early days - Sorrento Maternity Hospital, various boys' clubs, Centre 13 - no longer exist.

'94 opened with a programme of classical music at St Anne's, organised by Jeremy Ballard; Drama 13 were performing at Centre 13, there was an art exhibition at the Dovecote and a car boot sale at the Jug of Ale. Moseley Mastermind was replaced that year with the perhaps less terrifying Quiz Night.

1996 and 1997 were two great years for the Festival - Henrietta Lockhart and Jane Howell from Sage were in charge. The atmosphere was wonderful and bank balances were sound. But not for the first time I recall exhaustion setting in towards the end of the second year. Once again, Moseley people were expecting a Festival, but were much too busy to rally round and lend a hand. And did anyone detect Festival committee-members looking hopefully at Moseley Park that Autumn?

Rita Barker

Rita Barker's team took over in 1998 and took the huge step of moving the Festival from June (when it had always been) to the August Bank Holiday. And this was the year when Moseley Park, for so many years something of a mystery to many in Moseley, opened up its gates to the Festival. The weather was perfect (it had rained in June!) and the atmosphere tremendous - at last the Festival had some space.

But in 1999, even the usually indomitable Rita was moved to write that she was 'disappointed by lack of interest from a large percentage of organisations. . . . people should understand that the Festival helps to raise morale, promote economic growth'.

Jane Howell

But, given goodwill on all sides (including the neighbours!), the Park and the Festival should work well together in the future. And there's always the street-fair, the real back-bone of the event.

So, as this unique combination of street-fair, exhibition, song-fest, giant social and children's party approaches its thirtieth anniversary, the same tensions will doubtless continue; why will nobody lend us a hand?/what's happening to the Festival?/why don't they?/why me?

John Williams

LEISURE

CLASSICAL MUSIC

Moseley music is flourishing with musicians from the CBSO, freelance players, members of the now disbanded BBC Midland Radio Orchestra, music teachers, both school and private instrumental, highly talented non-professional musicians and, very importantly, a large audience of music lovers. Indeed, the CBSO undertook research in 2003 to identify ticket sales by postcode; up at the top of the list was B13.

Perhaps the most important effect of so many musicians living in one area has been on instrumental teaching, particularly for the young: from piano through violin to percussion, there will be a teacher. Some are schoolteachers, some private teachers and others, such as CBSO players, part time. This mix ensures a vast range of expertise not only in the teaching but also in organising small groups, when the need arises, such as for the young children's band, which ran for a while in the 1970s through to the young quartet which won the National Chamber Music Competition in 2004. From this culture, children have gone on to the National Youth Orchestra, music colleges, become professional players, international soloists and future audiences. This is a hidden but vital part of Moseley's musical life throughout the thirty years.

Beryl Chempin
Nationally renowned music teacher

Orchestral music has been varied, ranging from playing for fun or charity through to professional groups. Some have run for thirty years, others for only a few years. The Wednesday Band, formed by a Moseley music teacher, run from Moseley and containing many Moseley players, was founded in 1970 and is still going strong. Being a rehearsal orchestra and not giving concerts, it has provided music teachers, professionals, including those wishing to rehearse their concerti with an orchestra, and amateur musicians the chance to play through a large part of the classical repertoire. In contrast, The Moseley Sinfonia, also formed in the early 1970s by a group of CBSO players, gave public concerts to raise money for charity but is no longer functioning. The Messiah from Scratch, an annual event started in the 1980s, meets on the day for instant fun and fund raising. The most recent addition is the Sinfonia of Birmingham, formed in Moseley in 1994 and until recently rehearsing in Centre 13. A band of some forty players, a mixture of professional and non-professional players but with a professional leader and conductor, this small orchestra gives concerts around the Midlands and abroad, in 2004 touring in Italy.

Like teaching, chamber music has been an essential but, often, hidden part of the musical life; much of it takes place in people's homes purely for the pleasure of the participants. However, there have been some notable and long running Moseley based ensembles; The Midland Chamber Players, founded in 1966, are still giving around twelve concerts a year; The Arioso Quartet gave regular concerts until the 1990s from the inaugural concert in 1971 at Saint Anne's Church and, even now, gives an annual charity concert; Birmingham University Quartet was led for

John Joubert
Composer, long time resident in Moseley

years by a Moseley scientist. At the beginning of the twenty first century new groups are still forming, such as the Blenheim wind quartet and the Four Quarters string quartet.

Music performed in private homes is an excellent indicator of the health of the musical life and Moseley passes with flying colours. All over the area there are people meeting together to enjoy music; for the last twenty years an ad hoc group of up to twelve or so flautists has met every few months which has led to them performing at the British Flute Society Annual Meeting; another ad hoc group meets in a private house for the annual Mozart's Birthday Party celebrations. Music played by the old and young can be heard all over Moseley.

One of the delights and strengths of the last thirty years has been the continuous mixing of the professional expertise with the non-professional enthusiasm to create an exciting and lasting blend.

Elspeth Cox

LEISURE

MOSELEY SCOUTING

Looking back over the last 30 years, there have been have several significant changes in Scouting, not only nationally but also in Moseley.

Back in the early 1970s, Scouting was still getting used to its relatively new public image that had not only done away with the section names of Wolf Cubs, Boy Scouts, Seniors and Rovers but also the traditional khaki uniform and short trousers. The Scout Association had radically reorganised and updated the image of Scouting in this country introducing Cub Scouts and Scouts, and amalgamating the latter two older sections into Venture Scouts, with the option for them to become mixed units by including girls.

The uniforms and award systems were also updated to be more in keeping with the age, with even the traditional neckerchief initially changed for a tie for Ventures and Leaders.

Up until the national reorganisation scout groups in and around the area had all been part of Moseley District. However, the reorganisation of Birmingham Scout Association into districts based on compass points and a central 'Inner Birmingham' had seen imaginary lines drawn along Alcester and Stratford Road to form the basis of South district with South West and South East on either side.

All of these groups being active in such a small area shows that scouting was thriving during the 1970s, fuelled partly by the lack of other evening options for young people. The availability of adults was also crucial for the Movement's success, with people having time and a commitment to offering 'life skills' by way of fun and adventure to young people via a progressive training programme on meeting nights, day events, camps etc.

The locally based groups dramatically grew in the 1980's with the advent of Beaver colonies. This was a totally new section launched to encourage younger people from 6 years of age into Scouting and again it proved to be very popular around Moseley.

However, over recent years, the advent of other opportunities for young people, and a decline in adults coming forward as leaders have lead to a gradual fall in Scouting membership within Moseley, This is evident in the closure of sections or disbandment of whole groups over recent years.

Aware of these changing trends, two years ago leaders and parents at St. Agnes and St. Mary's scout groups took the bold decision to amalgamate and share their existing equipment and leadership resources so that they could continue providing quality scouting for young people in Moseley.

Creating a single Scout group supported by 80 local families has proved to be a great success for the Beaver colony, Cub pack and Scout troop who, since September 2004, have held meetings at St. Agnes Church Hall following the closure of Centre 13.

By way of going full circle, the last two years have also seen significant national changes within Scouting with new style uniforms, award schemes and the replacement of Ventures by Explorer and Network scouts. Meanwhile, the County of Birmingham is now reorganising itself and considering removing the imaginary lines that originally cut Moseley district into three.

In the next few years, we will be celebrating the Scout Associations' Centenary and the ideas that Robert Baden Powell had for creating a youth movement that would better prepare young people for their future. The recent changes by the Scout Association in general and in particular by leaders in Moseley have been designed to be relevant for today's young people while still holding true to his original values.

Chris Ball

LEISURE

THE STAGE

The definition of drama in the dictionary is the story of life and action for representation by actors; a dramatic situation or series of absorbing events. Another way of putting it is holding a mirror up to life. Over many years there has been plenty of drama in Moseley. As in most villages, it starts in the Church with the Nativity play depicting the birth of Christ or a tableaux representing it.

Moseley and District Council of Churches (MDCC), a group of actors whose main aim was to promote ecumenical understanding through drama, started in 1961. Membership was drawn from many people who belonged to various churches. I remember the *True Mystery of the Passion* in St Annes church and *Murder in the Cathedral* at St Marys. Sadly this group did not have a permanent home, but managed to work in and for churches. This dedicated group were taking theatre to the community, including the Fighting Cocks which was their home for years, when John Bradney and his very committed band of people decided to widen their scope with some classical drama. The problem was there was virtually no money to fund this – however Shakespeare needs no royalties, and an open air venue, which should not incur hire charges, would be ideal. One of their number was a resident of TOC.H in Wake Green Road. Here they had a large lawn and an overgrown orchard. Here in 1963 during a very wet summer, *A Midsummer Nights Dream* came to life in this magical setting and, although occasionally damp, this heralded the beginning of summer Shakespeare in Moseley.

The next step was to tour their productions which were held in many venues including the Botanical Gardens and Pembroke Castle which became fixtures and continue today. During the Summer of 2003 and 2004, Moseley Park became the hosts to two excellent productions of the *Taming of the Shrew* and *A Midsummer Nights Dream*. MDCC are still going strong and you would always be welcome. All you need is an interest in theatre. The contact name and number are Zeta Hall 0121-608 0579.

The Chameleon Theatre Company is a small, independent, amateur group which has been established for 21 years. They put on two productions a year, usually a full length play and a fifteen minute adaptation of a Shakespeare play or pantomime, both performed at MAC. The company, which prefers to produce comedies, has performed plays by Alan Ayckbourn, Tom Stoppard as well as children's plays such as *Gargling with Jelly* and *Kidnapped* at Christmas. They have also produced *Listen to This* by Michael Frayn, and an especially written fifteen minute version of Robin Hood. They always welcome new members, regardless of experience. They rehearse every Wednesday evening at 7.30 pm at the Warstock Community Centre. So do go along or contact them by e mail at liz@hensel.freeserve.co.uk or telephone 0121-449 5858.

Moseley Church of England Primary School had a PTA drama group, who put on productions to raise money for the school. After much hard work by many, many people, the Mini Theatre was created and St Marys Drama Group was reborn as **Drama 13** and has served the community since then, putting on two plays a year and a pantomime/childrens plays, staging everything from Aykbourn to Shaw and Coward to Wilde until August 2004. However, due to Centre 13 closing, sadly Drama 13 has become homeless. They will rise again – be sure. Several other groups have also used the centre to rehearse so they are also hoping that some community building will be found where a space to perform will be available.

Mix It's Theatre Company's mission is to produce amateur theatre at a professional standard. Their first play 'Exposed' was created by the cast and performed at MAC. The next piece was 'The Shape of Things' by Neil LaBute which was performed at the Moseley Dance Workshop in December 2004. For information on future productions please telephone Meriel Whale on 07946 488883.

The Villagers were a very dedicated and ambitious group, with very high standards, who performed classical plays and wrote their own material. They operated between 1975 and the early 90s. Their first production was the *Moseley Mysteries* written by Tony Shobrook. They performed in different venues including Churches and the Hexagon at MAC. I can remember some excellent productions that I saw. An adaptation of *Alice in Wonderland* and *Great Expectations,* some Chekov and plays by modern writers as well, including Michael Frayn. Some of the key figures in the group were Patti McGregor, Martin Pursey, Phillip Mahood, Jane Crabtree, Henry Eades, June Heather and Ella Lane who did a lot of the directing. The Villagers last production was *Alls Well that Ends Well* – they will be missed in Moseley.

Joan Taylor

LEISURE

HOW MOSELEY LOST ITS MOST FAMOUS INSTITUTION

It started with the money from Rupert Murdoch's News Corporation, the rivalry for exposure from Kerry Packer and the commercial potential of Jonah Lomu's playing talent - all these combined to initiate commercial Rugby Union in the Southern Hemisphere back in 1986.

In the Northern Hemisphere, Rugby Union clung to amateurism until it had no option but to launch itself headlong into the professional game. This was in 1995, and British Rugby was ill-prepared to produce an orderly transition. Clubs had to look after themselves and, inevitably, there emerged those who were able to raise sustained financial backing and those who could not.

Model of the 5000 seater stadium that never was

Moseley FC (Rugby Union) was founded in 1873 and had an illustrious history thereafter; the Club resolved that it had to compete in the professional game. Plans were drawn up to make the Reddings a 5,000-seater modern stadium, but opposition from Moseley residents prevented planning permission from being granted. In hindsight, perhaps the planning application was badly handled, or the opposition not far-sighted. Both may have been ill-informed; decisions were taken hurriedly on information that lacked substance, lack of knowledge resulting in attitudes that were perhaps too dogmatic. Decisions made then had unforseen and far-reaching results.

A consortium of Birmingham businessmen took over the Club, and the finance that they supplied not only stabilised matters but enabled Moseley to survive in National Division 2 in 1996-7. However, in the next season, immediate success was not forthcoming. The expected crowd support did not materialize despite the signing-up of several high-quality and charismatic players (and others who were over-valued). The consortium was obliged to put the Club into Administration in January 1998. The Reddings ground itself was sold to Bryants for housing development in the hope that the proceeds might be a contribution towards the purchase of a new ground suitable for the expectations of the professional era. Instead, after Administration, the proceeds went to cover outstanding debts, repayment of loans and some of the costs of preparing what has now become the new ground at Billesley Common.

Moseley played their last game at the Reddings on 6th May 2000 when they defeated Worcester, one of the clubs that was to find itself able to raise the finance needed in the modern game. Moseley had played their first game at the Reddings on October 6th, 1880, when they defeated Leicester. There followed 120 years of blood, sweat and tears and a peak of achievement when, at the height of Moseley's golden age in the 1970s, they were arguably the best club in the country.

A group of members endeavouring to ensure the Club's survival bought Moseley out of Administration in June 1998. It moved to the University of Birmingham, but was unable to obtain the long-term planning permission that would have enabled the Club to redevelop. Philanthropy without assets doesn't last for ever, and at the end of the 2001-2 season the Club was in danger of losing its Birmingham identity altogether. However, thanks to the generosity of many of its creditors, the help of Birmingham City Council - and yet another group of Club members who had enjoyed the cameraderie at the Reddings - Moseley found a new permanent home and, thus, the chance of a new and more hopeful beginning. Though now in the Second Division, they have survived - tradition has contributed to a resilience in the Club, both on and off the field.

Meanwhile, as we put together this account in the early Autumn of 2004, the Reddings pitch has been dug over, planning permission for housing has been granted, and Moseley Village has lost a distinguished sporting facility. All we can trust is that the new housing, and the people who will soon move in there, will enrich our community as much as Moseley Rugby Club had done over so many years. One last thought - at least Billesley Common is in Birmingham 13 postal district!

Peter Woodroofe

LEISURE

MOSELEY MUSIC

Moseley has long been a favourite haunt of many a professional, semi-professional - or amateur - musician. Many famous names have their musical roots in the area though, as is the case with Birmingham generally, Moseley has remained modest about its renowned sons and daughters. The artistic leanings and social gregariousness of Moseleyites in general has led to a wonderful atmosphere of creativity and keen partying spirit - sometimes not to the taste of all residents! - although there have always, for many reasons, been peaks and troughs.

Perhaps it would be best to start with some of the important factors affecting Moseley's musical life.

It must be said that the prosperous Victorians and Edwardians who built their grand residences here had a large hand in starting to make the pot bubble. By the 1950s, many of the large houses in the area were becoming too costly to maintain as family homes. Families who had grown up here had moved on to pastures new, leaving underused and difficult to manage, large, newly-empty houses.

Many of these houses were converted into flats and bedsits, which gradually attracted a population of students and artists from many cultural backgrounds, thus giving a steady flow of people both more receptive to new musical ideas, and also more inclined to be involved in making the music themselves - and all at a time in their lives when music mattered most.

This glorious period of mixed culture derived from popular music continued until the late 1990s but has been in decline for a while now, partially due to the success Moseley has had in recreating its earlier role as a pleasant residential suburb, the choice of - among others - many, now professional, successful artists and their young families. These young families however, may well provide the next link in Moseley's musical chain as we shall see when we look at some of the places and events that have shaped things over the last forty years or so.

Beside the bedsit/mixed culture/student explosion of the '60s to the '90s, we need to look in particular at some of the hotspots in the area.

Moseley Grammar School was something of a breeding ground for talent during the 1960s. The beat explosion of the early 60s, combined with more affordable electronic instruments, helped no doubt, but it cannot go unnoticed that a number of well-known musicians came from behind these school gates; names such as Frank Ifield, who had a few top 30 hits in 1962-3 (such as 'I remember you') and Jasper Carrott - mainly a comedian but also in groups, and who did have a novelty hit with 'Funky Moped' in 1975. Various members of the Moody Blues and the Electric Light Orchestra also passed through the School.

A potential new hotspot more recently might turn out to be Queensbridge School which has a wide musical curiculum - but we shall have to wait and see.

Licensed venues

Pubs, clubs and restaurants have all played their part; one of Moseley's best remembered live venues was the Fighting Cocks. Up to the mid-'80s, the large upstairs room was used for shows. Names that have passed into folk-lore trod the boards there during that time, including UB 40, Dexy's Midnight Runners, The Nightingales, The Beat, The Au Pairs, and so on. This really was Moseley's main venue during that time. Sadly, it then closed until the late 1990s, when bands might once again be heard, albeit in the lounge area downstairs. Even this came to an end when the ownership of the pub changed hands. But the Cocks remains a sleeping giant - with its history of entertainment, it must surely re-awaken one day.

Before the Dance Workshop on Alcester Road there was Cunninghams Cash Registers, and before them there was The Consort night club! Many distinguished names performed there, but the club experienced problems with local residents over their license due to noise (mostly departing customers!) When The Consort closed, true night-clubbing in Moseley came to an end.

For many years, the Trafalgar's upstairs function room was not in full-time use. But it did play host to a regular Sunday evening jam session. Trumpeter Duncan of Primal Scream was a regular player at these nights which were well attended by the locals. A similar folk music night on Wednesdays is still a feature in the pub, now renamed the Patrick Cavenagh. What's more, the upstairs function room was refurbished and reopened a few years ago. It is still thriving and has given birth to many now established promoters' nights. The Bull's Head only became a centre after its recent refurbishment, and now has live performances in its upstairs bar. It's now a thriving hot-pot of local talent. The Jug of Ale must, however, take pride of place in entertainment throughout the 90s and since. The building enlisted the services of Dave Travis as a promoter to bring in some of the biggest names in music. Performers such as Oasis (for £100!) and Ocean Colour Scene, to name but two, cut their musical teeth in the upstairs room there - and the pub has even hosted its own mini-festivals in the car park. The Jug now has a great reputation for live music on the Midlands circuit. Indeed Arthur Tap, now the main promoter at the Jug, is the son of the owners of the old Consort Night Club.

Though, strictly speaking, outside Moseley, the Moseley Dance Centre - formerly the Moseley and Balsall Heath Institute - has provided a late-night venue within walking distance for many years. And talking of fringe venues, there is evidence of a small stage and ballroom at 30 Wake Green Road - built at one time as an officers' club - which, though residential, still has its stage and polished dance floor!

The spirit of '70s Moseley, through to early '90s, could be found however in the many, legendary, house and garden parties which seemed to be happening around the Village most weekends. The large sub-divided Victorian and Edwardian homes were an ideal setting - for some pretty wild parties. The rambling multi-roomed nature of these properties allowed varied entertainments to go on in each room, with the garden providing yet another sound system and a makeshift bar!

Though strictly illegal, these garden and house parties, charging £1 entrance fee and selling beer from an open, ground-floor window, gave many people the source material for bigger, better-organised (and legal) gigs the world over. The spirit of Moseley is now international!

Recording studios

I know of only two commercial recording studios in Moseley; one is at the Dance Workshop on Alcester Road - a new facility - and the other is on Woodbridge Road and run by the Moseley impressario John Cotton. But, needless to say, there are many backroom studios busily recording the wealth of local talent. In the past, these small studios have been quite capable of producing hit or cult status records. Perhaps the most famous has been Bob Lamb's studio in his flat at 68 Cambridge Road. It was here that the then local, now global, group UB40 recorded their first album, 'Signing Off', produced by Bob himself. Legend has it that Bob had to go to the group's house at 212 Showell Green Lane (1 inch into Sparkhill!) to wake the group up and get them to his studio. Knowing that this no. 1 album was made in a local house gives it a whole new listening perspective.

Many less widely known but wonderful innovators have has their recording bases in Moseley including Pram, Higher Intelligence Agency, Swansway, and Brian Duffy, as well as the revered Stephen Duffy. Doubtless many more will follow.

Moseley Festival and Moseley Park

The main regular event to bring the community together has been the Moseley Festival. Over the last three decades, it has helped to provide a focal group for local performers, from Folk to Electronica. Performing on the streets or more recently in Moseley Park, this event has gained steadily in stature musically in recent years. Now that the Park is available, jazz musicians have come from all over the world to perform - such as in L'Esprit Manouche - adding greatly to the vibrancy of the area.

Music outlets

The opening of Jibbering Records on the Alcester Road has at last provided a non-pub based focal point for music. Not only can we find rare music from around the world but we can pick up current local recordings too.

Summary

With the creative industries' re-awakening in inner-city areas of Birmingham such as Digbeth, Moseley has lost a little of its musical importance. As a very popular residential area experiencing its own kind of regeneration, some of the creativity must inevitably be lost to areas more able to cater for the needs of musicians and audiences alike. However, while there may not be so many outlets here for live events, especially with the trend towards late opening of venues (Moseley venues are residentially 'land-locked'), it is likely that Moseley will remain Birmingham's bohemian haven, home to far more than its fair share of musical professionals.

Fuzz Townsend